THE DIVORCE BOOK

WHAT EVERY
MICHIGAN
MARRIED MAN OR WOMAN
NEEDS TO KNOW

THE DIVORCE BOOK

WHAT EVERY
MICHIGAN
MARRIED MAN OR WOMAN
NEEDS TO KNOW

...and 5 THINGS that can
sink your divorce case!

An informational guide
for MICHIGAN residents
concerned about the
consequences of divorce

ATTORNEY
Joseph T. Barberi

Printed in the United States of America.

ISBN: 978-1-59571-866-2
Library of Congress Control Number: 2013901037

$16.95

Designed and published by
Word Association Publishers

205 Fifth Avenue
Tarentum, Pennsylvania 15084

www.wordassociation.com
1.800.827.7903

TABLE OF CONTENTS

CHAPTER I
INITIAL CONSIDERATIONS

MARRIAGE COUNSELING

Before giving up on their marriage, most couples, and their children, will be best served by the couple committing themselves to work with an experienced marriage counselor to see if the marriage can be saved. Sometimes marriage counseling won't work, as either one spouse refuses to participate or domestic violence is ongoing. Accordingly, this book is written with the understanding that marriage counseling could not be attempted or has been tried and failed. That being said, at the first hint that a divorce is imminent, a spouse should begin to take action to protect himself/herself.

PROPERTY ISSUES

When it comes to the reason for divorce, I have found that the number one cause is money (e.g. "we don't make enough money to pay our debts"). The number two cause for divorce is money (e.g. "I don't like how you spend our money"). When it comes to dividing up what assets the parties have accumulated during the marriage, both spouses need to have access to all financial information pertaining to each spouse. This includes information regarding bank accounts, retirement monies, stocks, life insurance policies, etc. If one spouse has all the records, the other spouse should make an effort to secure "copies" of all important records. These include: individual and joint tax returns, business tax returns, balance sheets of solely owned businesses, monthly checking account records, etc. Once the divorce process starts, it may be much more difficult to secure documentation of all financial data. It is also possible that monies might be transferred from business accounts to phantom creditors, making it difficult to recover such monies later.

Depending on the unique facts of a spouse's situation and the type of business(es) involved, it may be extremely important to work early on with an experienced divorce attorney who has business relationships with financial experts. Such financial experts can offer assistance to the spouse in securing hard-to-obtain financial documentation **before** the other party becomes aware that initiation of a divorce is imminent.

TIP: "Disappearing" personal property issues: If there is any question that your spouse may try to hide personal property assets, such as tools, quads, boats, fishing equipment, guns, antiques, collectibles, etc., in essence any movable items of value, you should take photos and/or a video of such items before they disappear. If you have any indication that a divorce might be in the works (even months down the road), take these photos and/or a video as soon as possible. It's amazing how things suddenly "disappear" just before you file your Complaint for Divorce. If, however, you are contemplating moving out of the marital home anytime, i.e., to think things over, etc., I suggest that you take such photos and/or a video before you move out. Returning to the marital home to document what items of personal property were owned by the parties during the marriage can prove to be problematic.

CREDIT CARDS

Credit issues can also prove to be problematic, especially if both spouses can charge debts on joint credit cards or make draws on a joint line of credit. This is especially true when a joint line of credit is secured by a second mortgage on the marital home. Obviously, if a divorce appears likely, a spouse may wish to contact his or her credit card companies and, if a credit card is primarily in his or her name, stop the other spouse from having authority to make <u>further</u> charges. He or she may also stop the other spouse from making draws on a line of credit.

While a divorce court can apportion debt between spouses, a divorce court cannot require a bank or credit card company to shift debt between divorced spouses. Often, a bank has extended credit on a loan for a home based on the reported income of both spouses. In such a case, after divorce, one spouse might find herself awarded the marital house while the other spouse's name still remains on the underlying debt (e.g. promissory notes and mortgage). The bank may refuse to refinance the debt solely in the name of the person occupying the home. The refusal to refinance usually occurs because the spouse occupying the marital home has an insufficient income stream to justify the amount of mortgaged indebtedness. Accordingly, if a divorce is a possibility, spouses usually should not agree to jointly refinancing their home or other real estate before filing for divorce without first obtaining legal and financial advice as to the wisdom of such action.

Typically, as soon as one spouse files for divorce, the filing is "picked-up" by credit reporting agencies. Lending institutions receive regular credit reports reflecting such filings. Thereafter, many lending institutions are reluctant to extend credit to a spouse who does not have a high income level.

TIP: This point is especially **important for many women** who have been stay-at-home mothers, who typically have a significantly lower income level than their husbands. The stay-at-home mother (or the lower income spouse) may want to take out a credit card in his or her own name so that credit will be available to her or him after the divorce process starts; the farther ahead you plan and take action <u>before</u> the actual filing for divorce, the better situation you will have when it comes to credit issues.

CHAPTER II
LEGAL REPRESENTATION

DO I NEED AN ATTORNEY TO REPRESENT ME?

I am often asked whether a party actually *needs* an attorney to represent him/her in his/her divorce case.

ANSWER: In regard to whether a party needs an attorney to represent him/her in a divorce, my answer is simple— every Michigan citizen has the right to represent himself/herself in any type of litigation, including a divorce. If a party chooses to represent himself/herself, however, the court will hold that party to the same standard as if that party had gone to law school, passed the bar exam and been admitted to the state bar as a licensed attorney. Accordingly, **except in the simplest of cases**, there is a maxim that applies, to-wit: "A person who represents himself has a fool for a client." –Abraham Lincoln.

Simply put, if the marriage has been very brief; the parties have acquired no interest in real estate; have incurred no significant debt; have no retirement monies that need to be apportioned between them; have no need for receiving alimony or concerns about paying alimony; **and have no minor children where a custody arrangement, parenting time, or tax dependency allocations need to be addressed,** then, in such a "simple case," no attorney representation may be necessary. That would mean that the spouses can amicably divide their items of personal property—you take your car, I'll take my car–you take your clothes, I'll take my clothes–and each goes his or her own way. That type of a divorce is, indeed, a rare divorce. In such cases, there are do-it-yourself "divorce kits" available that can be filled out by a reasonably intelligent person who can follow instructions.

These divorce kits typically cost $150. An Internet search of do-it-yourself divorces in Michigan will reveal a number of sites where forms and step-by-step "instructions" can be found. Currently, court costs ranging from $150 to $230 usually are in addition to the cost of such divorce kits. Serving a summons and complaint on the other spouse is also an additional cost.

<u>Whenever minor children are involved, it is almost reckless for a spouse not to have legal representation.</u> When it comes to minor children, the parties' judgment of divorce will govern the children's movement back and forth between their mother and father until the youngest child of the marriage reaches 18 years of age.

> **TIP:** If a party is short on available funds and believes she can't afford to hire an attorney to represent her, she may request the assistance of a family law attorney to just "look over" a proposed judgment of divorce that has been prepared by the spouse's attorney. Remember, this written document (the judgment of divorce) will become the court's order that will govern custody and parenting time for the minor children for years to come. It would be much better to at least make sure that the judgment of divorce clearly spells out each spouse's rights when it comes to custody, parenting time, child support, and potentially the children's tax dependency allocation between the parents.

CAN ONE ATTORNEY REPRESENT BOTH SPOUSES?

I am also asked whether one attorney can represent both spouses in a divorce case and thereby save both spouses some of the expense of obtaining a divorce. When it comes to **the question** of whether one attorney can represent two spouses, my answer is very simple—**no**. It is ethically improper for one lawyer to "look out for the best interests" of both spouses. Obviously, what may be better for the wife may not be better for the husband when it comes to financial implications, eligibility for alimony or the obligation to pay alimony, property division, parenting time, and child support issues.

I tell all of my clients that it is always in everyone's best interests to have two experienced family law attorneys involved in the divorce process. Ultimately, it is easier for both parties if they each have attorneys who are looking out for their own individual interests, and in whom they can confide when discussing the many issues that arise in the divorce process.

WHICH ATTORNEY SHOULD REPRESENT YOU?

As soon as a spouse believes that a divorce might be possible, it is extremely wise for him or her to consider who he or she wishes to represent him or her should a divorce have to be started or be initiated by the other spouse. The "responding" party is usually at a disadvantage and has to "get up to speed" after the other spouse has filed for divorce. Usually the first party to file for divorce is more prepared since he or she has been advised on ways to gather important information to document his or her case before the divorce process starts. Additionally, "the best fit" for the spouse, in terms of legal representation, may already have become "unavailable" because the spouse's husband or wife may have already retained the legal counsel whom the other spouse might have desired, had she or he acted sooner.

TIP: If you have a particular attorney in mind that you might wish to retain or consult with regarding a divorce, don't mention his or her name to your spouse or to friends of your spouse. Friends of your spouse might confide to your spouse that "they heard" you were thinking of contacting a particular attorney about a divorce. I cannot tell you how many spouses have contacted me to represent them strictly out of concern, for whatever reason, that their spouses might retain me first. Instead, make an appointment to speak with the attorney you think you might wish to utilize if a divorce becomes necessary, and at least get a sense for whether you think such attorney would be a good fit for you.

Usually, the cost for an initial consultation is not high and the time is well spent obtaining some advice that is relevant to your unique situation. Every marriage is different and the unique facts of your case will result in advice particular to you, which cannot be given in this book.

Meeting with an experienced family law attorney early in the process can also pay dividends when it comes to connecting with the attorney's financial and investigative experts. Often family law attorneys have a particular business or real estate appraiser whom they enjoy working with and believe to be well received by judges in the local courts.

Contacting the attorney whom you think you might wish to have assist you, should a divorce be necessary, will also open you up to connections with the attorney's cadre of experts who could be utilized to help you. Such experts can help gather necessary information to document financial information or, in the case of inappropriate behavior, can help document the acts of your spouse that could affect his or her eligibility for alimony and/or receiving a 50/50 property split of the assets and debts involved in your marriage.

CHAPTER III

CUSTODY OF THE MINOR CHILDREN— MOVING OUT OF THE MARITAL HOME

Every couple who has children born by their union presents unique facts regarding what is in the best interests for their children after divorce. As the parties begin to separate their households, what type of custody arrangement (legal custody/ physical custody/joint or primary custody) and what parenting time schedule is believed to be best for their children may be something about which the parties have a strong disagreement. A more detailed discussion regarding the types of custody and parenting time arrangements is found later in this book.

TIP: Absent on-going domestic violence, I generally advise a party who believes that being awarded primary physical custody of the children is in the best interests of the children not to move out of the marital home. The children should sleep in their normal bedrooms and live where they have lived (near their school, neighborhood, and friends). If staying in the home is too stressful due to ongoing arguments (especially those that take place in front of the children), or if safety issues are present due to domestic violence or the mental instability of one of the spouses, then by all means move **out of the marital residence and take the children with you.** Again, if one party believes that he or she is the best parent to serve as the primary custodial parent, then, if at all possible, it is extremely important that such parent get sound legal advice from an experienced family law attorney well in advance of the start of the divorce process.

Although it's not always possible, since sometimes a startling event may precipitate the filing of the divorce, it is always much better if the party wishing to gain primary physical custody of the parties' minor children has time to plan the process.

CHAPTER IV

WHERE WILL THE DIVORCE ACTION TAKE PLACE?

Critical issues, such as venue (the county in which the divorce complaint is filed,) can dramatically affect the outcome of the parties' custody case. The party who receives the earliest and best legal advice often obtains a major advantage in the divorce process. It is important to know that there are 83 counties in Michigan, each with different Friend of the Court offices, who can have different policies and personnel.

The "Friend of the Court" is an individual appointed by the Chief Circuit Court Judge of the county in which the Friend of the Court will serve. The Friend of the Court is in charge of monitoring staff assigned to the Friend of Court's Office, who are charged with assisting parties in the family court system.

Each county's Friend of the Court Office has a staff of individuals assigned to process child custody matters between parents involving their minor children, including making recommendations as to child support.

The Friend of the Court may also serve as a referee, or appoint a member of the Friend of the Court staff to serve as a referee to initially hear disputes between parties and to recommend orders to the family law judges. Their recommendations typically become the orders of the court, unless objected to by one of the parties within the time allotted for such objections to be made. More information will be detailed later in this book regarding the Office of the Friend of the Court and options to opt-out of Friend of the Court services.

Accordingly, which county is selected to be the county where the complaint for divorce is filed will determine which Friend of the Court's office (and which Friend of the Court's policy manual for custody and parenting time) will govern the custody process in the divorce case. In many cases, a divorce case could be filed in either of two different counties based on where the parties reside. If one spouse has already moved out of the marital home and has established a residence in another county for ten days, then that spouse may file the complaint for divorce in that county or in the county where the other spouse continues to reside.

Again, obtaining legal advice on important custody issues can have a profound effect on the outcome of a party's custody and parenting time arrangement. There are many do's and don'ts when it comes to a party's custody and parenting time case and understanding that ultimately they are based on what's best for the children.

Documentation of who has been the children's primary care-giver can be extremely important when it comes to "proving in court" who did or did not do what. Often, testifying can boil down to a "he says/she says" dispute.

TIP: Having objective documentation from third parties often carries the day in court. Records of text messages, videos, and tape recordings can be helpful or harmful. Accordingly, all the things you do or don't do shortly before a divorce is filed, or even shortly after a complaint for divorce has been filed, can have a tremendous impact on the outcome of your custody case, as well as your divorce case in general.

5 THINGS THAT CAN SINK YOUR DIVORCE CASE

5 THINGS THAT CAN SINK YOUR DIVORCE CASE:

1) No matter what is said or done by your spouse, no matter "what buttons are pushed," DO NOT and I repeat DO NOT allow your temper to cause you to physically harm your spouse or even worse, your children. Not only is a physical injury to your spouse or children a criminal matter, possibly causing you to face public prosecution for your actions, but physical violence can also have profound ramifications on your divorce case. Domestic violence and emotional abuse can serve as a basis for a Personal Protection

Order being entered by the court (commonly known as a PPO). Having a PPO entered against a spouse can have a major impact on who stays or leaves the marital home and on who obtains primary custody of the parties' minor children. It can also be a factor as to whether alimony is awarded and whether a 50/50 property division is ordered.

2) If you want to pursue primary physical custody, DO NOT, I repeat DO NOT, move out of the marital home without taking the minor children with you. "Leaving the home" where your children have lived for a significant period of time, without taking the children with you, will often be viewed as a form of abandonment. If there is physical violence in the home, either leave with the children or seek sound legal advice from an experienced family law attorney. You may be able to obtain an ex parte order granting you exclusive use of the marital home or be referred to a shelter where you and your children can reside temporarily. Obtaining an order "*ex parte*" means that you obtained the order without your spouse even knowing that you've filed for divorce and your spouse was not allowed to participate in the court's *initial* decision.

The underlying facts that support your request for exclusive use of the marital home, if such an order is to be granted *ex parte*, need to be compelling and present a picture of the potential physical harm to you or your children that could occur should the *ex parte* order not be granted. Otherwise, a request for exclusive use of the marital home will need to be made at a court hearing *after* your spouse has been given an opportunity to respond to your accusations. If domestic violence is a concern, there are shelters available where abused parties, most often women, can reside with their children. Such an option may be available to you in your particular county and by consulting with an experienced family law attorney; you will have this information provided to you.

3) If you have become romantically involved with a third party, don't bring the third party "into the marriage" before filing for divorce. Additionally, if there are minor children involved, don't introduce the third party to the children until a lengthy time has elapsed *after* the divorce process has started.

Often, the marriage has "broken down" long before one party actually files for divorce. This delay in time is often when spouses, feeling alone in their marriage, find themselves attracted to someone else "who listens to them" or "who understands," and things happen.

When they do, don't make the mistake of waiting too long to file for divorce, otherwise your "affair" may be used against you for causing the breakdown of the marriage when property division and alimony issues arise. Accordingly, when child custody, property division, and alimony issues are being decided, don't make your "affair" the focus of discussion.

Exposing children to a new boyfriend or girlfriend before a complaint for divorce is filed can be emotionally devastating to minor children. If litigated, I can assure you that the court will hold it against the spouse who makes the mistake of introducing the girlfriend or boyfriend to the children too early in the separation process. As soon as possible, obtain good legal advice on how to deal with the development of your involvement with a third party. You should also obtain advice as to how to best tell your children about the divorce and about any relationship by one of the spouses with a third party.

TIP: If at all possible, have both spouses sit down together with the children and tell the children about the divorce. During such discussion, make sure that the children know that they are not responsible for the break-up of their parents. A video entitled "Start Making It Livable for Everyone (**SMILE**)" is available to help educate parties on how to treat children during the divorce process. After a party's initial consultation with an experienced family law attorney, a viewing of the "SMILE" video can usually be arranged by the attorney in the attorney's office. Many counties require viewing this video as part of the court's divorce process.

4) Don't tell your children how bad their father or mother is, no matter what their father or mother did to you. All children typically want to love both parents; even though what your spouse did may have been wrong, don't be the messenger of such information.

When it comes to a child custody dispute, Michigan's best interest, factor (J), "the willingness and ability of each of the parties to facilitate and encourage a close and continuing parent-child relationship between the child and the other parent or the child and the parents," can be an important factor. The factor will be weighed against a parent who "bashes" the other parent to their children. As stated, it is emotionally harmful for children to hear about the poor choices of their fathers or mothers and the worst way for them to hear about these matters is one parent bad-mouthing the other. Resist the temptation to "spill the beans" to the children. Excuses like, "I'm just being honest with them," "they deserve to know what's going on," or "I need to tell them so they understand why things have changed" are not justifiable reasons to speak to or in front of the children about the other parent's shortcomings. Children don't need to know anything regarding the bad actions of their mothers or fathers unless that parent is posing a risk to them, e.g., if a father or mother has physically or sexually abused a child, or has mental health issues causing them to place the children in harm's way.

If you can, spare your children from knowing about the misbehavior of the parent whose actions have hurt you, and instead take the high road by keeping mum on the issue as to what the other parent did. In the long run, you will be rewarded not only by the court, but more importantly, by your children. Your children will continue to love and respect you even more for not tearing down their image of their other parent and in time, they'll sort things out for them-selves—trust me.

5) DO NOT, I repeat DO NOT post anything on Facebook® about yourself or your spouse. Also DO NOT text anything to your spouse or one of your spouse's friends that you do not wish to be introduced against you in your divorce case as "Exhibit 1."

In our social digital world, we freely exchange information about ourselves, our friends, our spouses, or our new romances. It continues to amaze me how many individuals do not realize that spouses who are upset with their partners will save these "comments" for use in court. Trust me, such postings and texts will come back to haunt the offending party and will become potential exhibits to be introduced at trial.

If you've already posted something harmful, delete it as soon as possible. Even after you've deleted such postings, technical experts may be able to retain or retrieve such deleted postings. Accordingly, the best policy is never to post, text, or email anything in the first place that could be harmful to your case because, as I stated, it will come back to haunt you if your case is litigated in court.

CHAPTER VI
CONFIDENTIAL COMMUNICATIONS

When you consult with your lawyer regarding the unique facts of your marriage, it is imperative that you tell your family law practitioner all of the good and all of the bad about yourself and your marriage. I can assure you that all of bad will likely come out in your divorce case from your spouse.

If you have not alerted your family law attorney as to the bad that might come out, then he or she will not be able to position you in the best possible way for when this information comes out. It is much better to admit upfront to the family law judge that you have made mistakes than to have your spouse use your mistakes to cast you in a negative light. For example, denying an affair can make you susceptible to a perjury charge, and a judge could also conclude that you have been dishonest about other matters.

Regarding third parties, the best course of action is to file for divorce *before* you start a relationship with another person. If you believe your marriage is over, and you realize that you are attracted to another person, it is better to file for divorce *before* allowing your attraction to develop into a sexual relationship.

TIP: Men and women view "affairs" differently. Most men tend to think that as long as they haven't had sex with their paramour, they aren't having an affair. For a woman, however, it's different. If her husband is confiding in another woman, an "emotional affair" is taking place. Such an emotional affair is, to many women, just as bad as if their husbands were having a sexual affair with another, because their husbands are breaching the trust relationship. As such, the wife may maintain that it was her husband's "emotional affair" with another woman that caused the breakdown of the marriage.

Tell your attorney with whom you consult everything–so that he or she can properly advise you. That is why spiritual leaders, medical personnel, and lawyers all have statutory and common law confidentiality protections available to you, so that anything you say to your lawyer, your doctor, or your spiritual leader can remain confidential. We have these protections available so that the penitent, the patient, and the client can all know that their confidential communications to their professional advisors (including their marriage counselors), will remain confidential and not be revealed to others without their permission. Keep in mind, however, whatever you tell your mother/father/brother/sister/best friend is *not* confidential.

TIP: Having a "supportive" person in the room with you when you consult with your attorney can also cause your privilege against disclosure of what you say to your attorney to be compromised. Accordingly, if there are sensitive issues to be discussed, you may ask that your mother/father/brother/sister/best friend be excused from your consultation with your attorney.

CHAPTER VII
EMOTIONAL ASPECTS OF DIVORCE

Most people view divorce as a way to rid themselves of a bad marriage. They do not realize that divorce itself creates deep emotional feelings. Before making a decision to divorce, spouses should give careful consideration to the consequences of divorce. Counseling can help with the pros and cons of the divorce decision. There are many good counselors located throughout Michigan, who help persons with marriage/divorce issues.

A significant percentage of clients who come into my office to discuss a divorce have not actually decided to file for divorce. First, they want to know their options. I typically encourage them to explore alternatives, including counseling, and, depending on their circumstances, I suggest options as to how they can protect themselves and meet their needs, short of divorce.

In Michigan, a divorce can be obtained without a determination of fault. Most divorce cases never go to trial. Divorce cases are "civil" as opposed to "criminal" cases, and when it comes to the division of assets and debts acquired during the marriage,  they are similar to cases involving the dissolution of a business partnership. While similarities do exist with other types of civil cases, issues involving children and intimate conduct between the parties make divorce cases some of the most emotionally charged cases that pass through the judicial system.

Despite the fact that most divorces are settled out of court, it is also important to realize that the break-up of a marriage is a legal dispute between a husband and wife where each spouse attempts to have his or her point of view prevail. This atmosphere of conflict often interferes with attempts to reach an agreement on issues regarding property settlement, alimony, child support, and parenting time. Reaching an agreement on issues involving children reduces future conflict in court and reduces trauma for the children.

There are stages in a divorce leading to emotional acceptance of the end of the marriage. No matter how difficult the marriage, the act of getting married creates an emotional bond between the wife, the husband, and the children. Each person goes through stages before he/she can accept the emotional consequences of a divorce and begin a new life. Each of these stages has a great deal to do with how a divorce will proceed. Long-term emotional, financial, and legal consequences can result if these feelings are not dealt with before, during, and after a divorce.

BEFORE THE DIVORCE

Consulting with an experienced family law attorney can provide spouses with an objective professional assessment of how their feelings may affect their cases. For example, a spouse who denies the possibility of a divorce may feel he/she should "give the other spouse everything" hoping that the divorce will "blow over." Acting on this feeling may create difficult emotional and financial problems down the road. Another problem occurs when a spouse says, "I just want to get the divorce over with," based on feelings of hopelessness and despair. He/she may concede all of the marital assets in an effort to rid himself/herself of the uncomfortable feelings associated with the divorce process. Reactions like these are a normal part of the divorce process.

When children are involved, parents need to realize that there will be a continuing relationship with their spouse for years to come, at least until their youngest child reaches the age of 18. During the divorce process and even after the youngest child attains the age of 18, children and ex-spouse issues continue with marriages, grandchildren, and medical-related issues of adult children. While the children are under 18, you will continue to meet your spouse frequently while exchanging the children for parenting time. Children going through the process of divorce experience as many difficult emotions as their parents. Divorce for the children creates feelings of self-doubt and worthlessness. It is crucial for children to understand that they are not the cause of a divorce. Some children blame themselves for causing their parents to divorce. It is also crucial for parents to understand that it is next to impossible to keep marital problems hidden from the children.

Although the wife and husband are ending their legal and emotional ties, these same people will be their children's parents for life. Parents can benefit from therapy to help them understand their children's needs when a family is breaking up. Children also need an opportunity to grieve the loss of their family as an intact unit. Recognizing the children's emotional loss is important, even when the divorce is in the best interests of the children. Accordingly, decisions about how to approach a divorce should be made with them in mind. The age and maturity of the child impacts how the child will adjust to his or her parents' divorce. Accordingly, it is worthwhile for parents to educate themselves about this issue and to consider each child's development and the best way to help each child process the impact of the parental divorce—before, during and after the divorce. Decisions about how to approach a divorce should be made with the children in mind.

TIP: In some cases, it might be necessary for children to counsel with a therapist to work out some of the fear, guilt, loss, and negative feelings caused by the break-up of their parents' marriage.

DURING THE DIVORCE

LENGTH OF TIME

In cases *not* involving minor children, once the complaint for divorce has actually been filed with the court, the waiting period is 60 days. For cases involving minor children (under 18 years), the waiting period is 180 days. However, a portion of the 180 days may be waived by the court for good cause (spousal abuse, child molestation, one parent leaving the country for military service, etc.), but *only* if the 60-day waiting period has expired. Cases not involving minor children typically resolve in four to six months. If a great amount of assets is involved, however, such cases can drag on for six months to one year.

Cases involving minor children typically take between seven and nine months to resolve. If the parties are arguing about their custody arrangement or parenting time, however, then such cases can take easily take ten months to one year to resolve, and each county is different depending on the county's caseload. Custody disputes are generally the most costly to the parties, both in terms of emotion and in terms of dollars spent on attorney fees and court costs.

At the beginning of a lawsuit, it is difficult to foresee how long each case will take to complete. After it is underway and many of the issues unfold, most experienced family law attorneys should be better able to gauge the expected duration.

How long the process will take depends on a combination of the following factors:

a) The number and complexity of *contested* issues;

b) The vehemence of the parties' feelings and their inclination to settle;

c) The court's calendar. A hearing can usually be scheduled within 30 days. A full divorce trial, which can take days to complete, usually must be scheduled three to six months in advance;

d) The other spouse. Is the other spouse arguing about custody and parenting time to gain leverage on the parties' property settlement? Is the other spouse arguing about parenting time just to argue or because he or she believes that his or her position is in the children's best interests? Is the spouse refusing to agree to anything in the hopes that by dragging out the process he or she might save the marriage or punish the other spouse? Any of these issues may affect your and your attorney's ability to move the divorce along without consternation and emotions running high;

e) The other lawyer. No attorney has control over the other attorney's schedule or personality. An extremely busy or uncompromising opposing counsel can prolong a divorce and add to your and your spouse's legal costs.

By far, the most common factor that prolongs lawsuits is the intensity of the parties' feelings and the degree to which parties want to argue or bicker. A good family law court system, where parties can express their feelings and have an opportunity to be heard, helps the process run much more smoothly. It's up to family law judges in each county to develop such a system where emotionally charged issues, involving what is best for minor children, receive the time and attention they deserve.

Sadly, some counties allocate very few resources to help divorcing spouses with their issues. Having a Friend of the Court hearing before a Referee to "temporarily decide" where the parties' minor children will reside during the divorce process (i.e. for the next four to ten months) is a critical hearing. Many witnesses can be called in support of each party's point of view. Yet in some counties, because of the county's allocation of resources, the Friend of the Court Referee is only allowed to schedule a one- or two-hour hearing for both parties to "make their cases" for what parenting time arrangement they believe is best for their minor children. In other counties, however, you are allowed to schedule a one-, two-, or three-day Referee hearing. Which county do you think allows the parties a better opportunity to make their respective cases regarding custody and parenting time issues?

Obtaining an unfavorable decision from the Referee, from one spouse's point of view, is usually handled much better if the spouse believes that he or she had a fair opportunity to present his or her witnesses and to be heard. There are also legal issues involved regarding what is known as a "*de novo*" hearing and who can or cannot be called as a witness in a contested custody case after the Friend of the Court hearing. Obtaining good legal advice on this issue is county and fact specific and needs to be obtained from an experienced family law practitioner familiar with the local family court judges, their policies, and their procedures.

In Isabella County, where I often practice, we have a very good system. An initial meeting with the Friend of the Court Referee takes place to see if the parties, with their counsel, can work out an acceptable custody and parenting time arrangement. If no agreement has been reached, absent unusual circumstances, the referee typically takes limited testimony from just the parties and then recommends a temporary custody and parenting time order. This recommended order will become the order of the court unless one of the parties objects to the same within 21 days. If either party objects to the temporary order, then a formal hearing is scheduled. Typically, the formal hearing will be held within 60 days and witnesses in addition to the parties may be called upon to testify. The formal hearing could last for one to three days, depending on the number of witnesses and the complexity of the issues involved.

The Friend of the Court Referee works with the parties and their attorneys to schedule the formal hearing, which allows both parties ample time to present their case for why they believe a particular custody/parenting time arrangement is in the best interests of the parties' minor children. Giving the parties and their attorneys this time settles 90% of custody cases. Parties and their witnesses are called and cross-examined, just as they would be called at trial before the family law judge assigned to their case. If either party does not agree with the decision of the Friend of the Court Referee, he or she can object and request that a *de novo* hearing be scheduled to be heard before the family law judge at a later date.

AFTER THE DIVORCE

Many people are shocked after their divorces when they find themselves still involved in emotional conflicts with their ex-spouses. Although a divorce can be obtained by one spouse, "a good divorce," like a good marriage, takes the cooperation of both parties. Some ex-spouses do not resolve their feelings until years after the divorce is final.

If you are caught in this type of conflict, be aware that there are services available to help you create a good divorce, either through counseling or with the help of a mediator. Some of these services may be available through your county's Friend of the Court's office.

Spouses gain no advantage in depriving their ex-spouses of what they are entitled to receive. The approach that will help resolve post-divorce conflicts is always to start a conversation by recognizing the other person's concerns and thereafter, stating your concerns. Then, see if both spouses can find some common ground. Normally, both parties should try to seek a compromise in their position that is workable under the circumstances.

CHAPTER VIII
FINANCIAL ASPECTS OF DIVORCE

It is difficult to estimate realistically the total cost of each divorce, even when your lawyer knows the issues that will be contested and the strength of the parties' feelings. If spouses do not trust each other, want complete discovery of all assets and liabilities, and argue many issues to the bitter end, the process will be long, drawn out, and expensive. Going to trial is almost always more expensive than settling the lawsuit. Going to trial usually only occurs when one or both parties are being unreasonable.

I have been involved in a number of what are referred to as "high-end divorces" involving millions of dollars to divide. With an experienced family law attorney representing the other spouse and with both spouses being reasonable, most of these cases have settled with little acrimony and without a lot of legal fees being incurred by the parties (and without a trial).

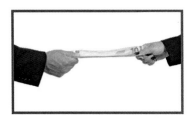

On the other hand, even with a good family law attorney "on the other side," my client and I have been "forced to litigate" cases. On occasion, one spouse tries to bully the other spouse into taking a settlement that the other spouse (and his or her attorney) believes to be totally unfair. This leaves the responding spouse with no real choice at all, other than to try the case. For this reason, we have family law judges to make decisions. In my experience, when this happens, a good trial attorney will expose the bullying spouse and make the unreasonable spouse regret his or her actions in forcing a trial. My clients and I have been forced to try cases where we obtained decisions awarding my clients hundreds of thousands of dollars "above" what my clients would have settled for in order to avoid a trial. While the legal expenses will be higher and emotionally draining for clients, the outcome will usually be worth trying the case rather than accepting a totally unfair "final offer."

In such regard, I have tried cases where the court decisions have resulted in awards to my client of over $1 million more than their spouses had "offered" to settle the case. A spouse, often the woman, has only one opportunity to obtain a fair division of marital assets and if this means having to go to trial to obtain it, then so be it. Again, that is why the legal system is utilized as the final arbitrator between parties dissolving their financial relationship. Accordingly, good family law attorneys need to be good trial attorneys so that in the event that a case must be tried, each spouse has an attorney who is confident in going to court to present the equities of a client's respective position.

Divorce can have a dramatic impact on the financial circumstances of one or both parties to a divorce, as well their children. It is not unusual for the standard of living for all concerned to drop considerably in the aftermath of a divorce. And, as has been frequently reported, this is more often a problem facing the parent who is awarded custody of the children, typically the mother, and who is either not working or is making considerably less than the non-custodial parent (more often than not, the father).

Even where there are no minor children at home, divorce can have a devastating financial effect on middle-aged and older divorcing parties, especially if they have been out of the work force for some time and have limited job skills and experience. In addition, frequently one spouse has attended to most of the couple's financial affairs, often leaving the other ill equipped to manage the vast array of financial matters of the family.

Thus, it is important for divorcing parties, particularly those living on limited budgets and who have little experience handling financial affairs, to be aware of the various matters that need to be addressed and to take appropriate action. This section highlights items that should be considered by parties to a divorce during the following phases:

1. Before an anticipated divorce begins;

2. During the divorce proceedings; and

3. After the divorce.

These items should not be viewed as all-inclusive. Every marriage is unique and may present needs not common to most divorces. While many of the items listed below will be more helpful to the spouse with less financial experience and economic independence, they are intended to serve as a master checklist to be used by anybody facing divorce.

GATHERING INFORMATION

Assemble as much information as possible regarding family financial matters. Include copies of tax returns for the last three years; lists of marital assets and debts such as are often required for credit applications; wills, trusts, and estate planning schedules and documents; the most recent statement from your spouse's employer regarding employee fringe benefits, especially retirement pensions; and recent account statements from financial institutions such as banks, credit unions, and brokerage houses.

MODIFY ESTATE PLANNING/
LIFE CARE DOCUMENTS

As a spouse begins the divorce process, the first order of business should be to review his or her will and make appropriate changes. If he or she does not have a will, it is generally advisable to have a lawyer prepare one now or immediately after the divorce, otherwise intestate succession laws may conflict with your wishes. Sadly, I am aware of clients who died during the divorce process and their estranged spouses took almost everything under an "old" will that was not changed. Changing the will is especially critical if it is the spouse's second or third marriage, where the death could possibly result in leaving all of the spouse's assets to his or her estranged spouse and excluding the deceased spouse's own children. If a spouse owns property in another state, they will likely benefit from the establishment of a trust.

It may be even **more important** to review any power of attorney that has been previously executed. Health care powers of attorney appointing one spouse to be the patient advocate for the other usually no longer make any sense. For example, why would the wife want her estranged husband to make the call in a trauma situation as to whether to "pull the plug" if she is injured and in a coma?

TIP: At the beginning of the divorce process, I normally recommend making or modifying a previous general durable power of attorney for financial matters and a durable health care power of attorney appointing a patient advocate to make medical healthcare decisions if the person should become incapacitated. If needed, I typically recommend appointing a parent, sibling, or trusted adult child to carry out these responsibilities.

ECONOMIC INDEPENDENCE

TTake steps to establish some measure of economic independence. Establish a bank account in your own name and put away as much money as possible. If you do not have credit in your name, apply for a credit card and make payments on a timely basis. It is often easier to start with a department store or gasoline credit cards before applying for major credit cards like Visa and MasterCard. Do not incur any additional joint debt with your spouse. If you are currently working, remain employed. Make needed repairs on major appliances, cars, etc., out of joint family funds. Also, take care of all of your medical and dental needs out of family funds.

TIP: Under current social security rules, a marriage must last for **ten years** for a spouse to be eligible to receive social security benefits based on the other spouse's earnings history. This is especially important for **women**, since women often have an earning history, income-wise, substantially lower than their husbands' earning history. Accordingly, if your marriage is close to the ten-year mark, you may want to delay starting or completing your divorce until your marriage has lasted for at least ten years.

MEASURES OF PRECAUTION

When divorce is likely, it is advisable to take prudent actions. Do not sign any joint income tax returns if you have reason to believe they have not been properly completed. Notify financial institutions where you have joint accounts of the possible divorce and request that no large transactions be permitted without joint approval of both spouses. Close out joint charge accounts, or, if you want to retain them, notify the creditors in writing that you will no longer be responsible for your spouse's purchases. If you are covered under the health insurance of your spouse's employer, verify that your coverage has not been terminated by your spouse.

DURING THE DIVORCE

When divorce proceedings begin, first review the items listed above and make sure that you have taken every precaution. Also, bear in mind that much of the advice applicable to the time before the divorce, applies equally after the proceedings have begun.

Prepare a budget of expenses, on both an annual and monthly basis, for you and your children (if any). Give this budget to your attorney to use as a basis for requesting temporary financial support from your spouse and negotiating adequate future financial support for you in the final Judgment of Divorce (alimony).

Make sure that, where appropriate, your divorce settlement includes provisions for:

1. alimony;

2. child support (including child care costs);

3. health insurance for the children, possible group health care coverage for spouses under COBRA (up to 3 years after the divorce);

4. division of responsibility for children's medical and dental expenses not covered by insurance;

5. division of property interests, including any pensions or other retirement benefits (utilizing a QDRO, EDRO, etc.);

6. appropriate security and life insurance protection to ensure the continued payment of financial support ordered and any installment payments of property division;

7. responsibility for debts of the marriage, including mortgage payments and property taxes during the pendency of the divorce;

8. responsibility for any contingent liabilities (such as tax deficiencies that may be assessed from previously filed tax returns);

9. division of any income tax refunds to be received, entitlement to claim dependency exemptions on future income tax returns, payment of legal fees, and payment for any special educational or other expenses of the children (for example, psychological therapy, college education, etc.)

Keep in mind that college expenses of children usually *cannot* be ordered by the court unless both parties agree to make such obligation part of *their* property settlement. Also, keep in mind that while a group health insurance plan may be available to the non-employee spouse under COBRA, the monthly cost for such a policy is usually very expensive and the party being covered may be required to pay for such expense.

AFTER THE DIVORCE

INSURANCE

Make every effort to be sure that your health insurance coverage will remain uninterrupted. Where you do not independently have such coverage by reason of your employment, continued coverage under your spouse's employer's coverage may be available under the provisions of a federal law known as COBRA.

In 1985, Congress passed the Consolidated Omnibus Budget Reconciliation Act (COBRA). COBRA applies to employers of 20 employees or more. Accordingly, COBRA coverage may not be available to an employee's spouse in a small group health plan. If applicable, within 60 days of entry of the parties' judgment of divorce, the non-employee divorced spouse must give the plan administrator for the health group of the divorced spouse's employer "notice" of the non-employees spouse's desire to have access to coverage under the former spouse's employer's group health plan. Such notice must be mailed (and post marked) within the applicable time frame.

Additionally, consider your own life insurance and disability insurance needs. Make appropriate changes in beneficiary designations on retirement benefits or any insurance that is presently in force. Make sure to check periodically that your former spouse is currently paying premiums on any insurance he or she is required to maintain under your divorce settlement as security for support or other payments to you.

VARIOUS TAX AND FINANCIAL MATTERS

For the divorced spouse who did not deal with tax and financial matters during the marriage, a number of new responsibilities must be assumed. Estimated income taxes may have to be filed quarterly, especially by spouses receiving alimony. It is often advisable for the newly divorced spouse to hire a tax advisor to help him or her with tax matters that arise in the divorce process and in the transitional year after divorce.

TAX DEDUCTIONS FOR ALIMONY PAYMENTS

When figuring your yearly tax liability after divorce, a determination needs to be made of what expenses are deductible to the payor as alimony and what payments are taxable as alimony to the payee. Many items other than those clearly labeled "alimony" may be deductible to one spouse and taxable to the other. Such items may include the home mortgage payments, utility payments made by one spouse for the residence of the other, real estate tax payments, auto loans, and even some uninsured medical bills. The status of these items as deductible or taxable depends on the individual circumstances of your case. A good family lawyer or C.P.A. will be happy to explain the tax ramifications to a spouse in his or her individual situation.

DEPENDENCY EXEMPTIONS

WHO GETS THE EXEMPTION

A major tax consideration in any divorce involving dependent children is determining which spouse will claim the dependency exemptions. In negotiating a divorce settlement, the value of the deduction must be figured and then a decision must be made by a spouse's attorney on how to structure the settlement to best accomplish what is desired.

There are several factors that must be weighed in determining which spouse will have the right to take the exemption. These factors include which parent has had custody of the child for the majority of the year and how much support each parent has provided. The general rule is "the custodial parent is entitled to the exemption." Generally, the parent who has had custody of the child the greater portion of the year is the "custodial parent." Michigan's child support formula "assumes" the primary custodial parent is taking the exemption.

RELEASING THE DEPENDENCY EXEMPTION

Although the custodial parent is generally allowed to claim dependent children as tax exemptions, the Internal Revenue Service provides an opportunity for the custodial parent to release the exemption to the non-custodial parent through a written agreement. Form 8332 provides the custodial parent with the means to release exemption claims. Form 8332 is designed to allow a release of the exemption for a single year, a designated number of years, every other year, or permanently.

Generally, I recommend that Form 8332 be filed each year depending on the status of child support payments. If the spouse paying child support to the custodial parent is not in arrears in making support payments, the release of the exemption may be offered to the spouse paying the child support with the condition that any net tax savings will be split between the spouses. This provides incentive for the spouse paying the support to remain current with support payments and both spouses enjoy the tax savings of the exemption.

OTHER TAX CAUTIONS

Always be cautious about signing a joint tax return that you believe may not be accurate. No spouse should sign a tax return that he or she believes might be incorrect or fraudulent. If a spouse signs the tax return, the spouse can be held completely responsible for any taxes, interest, and penalties that may accrue because of an inaccurate return.

THE INNOCENT SPOUSE RULE

While a former spouse's income tax liabilities can unexpectedly plague the other spouse even years after a final divorce, there is one protection provided by the Internal Revenue Code for spouses who had no knowledge of the inaccuracies. In a situation where the IRS is attempting to hold one spouse responsible for the other spouse's tax liabilities, the innocent spouse may escape responsibility if he or she can prove that he or she did not know of and had no reason to know of the erroneous items. This is a difficult burden of proof to meet. The easier path would be to do everything you can to ensure that the tax forms are complete, honest, and accurate.

ALIMONY RECAPTURE

Under the Internal Revenue Code, alimony, by definition, must be periodic and made in discharge of a legal obligation arising from a marital or family relationship. Child support, property divisions, and voluntary payments are not allowed the tax deductibility that is permitted for alimony.

If alimony is made in a lump sum payment, it may not be considered to be alimony, but rather a property division, and will lose its tax deductibility to the payor. The IRS has developed a complicated formula to determine whether alimony can be paid out in a manner that allows tax deductibility. If the formula shows that the alimony is paid out too heavily in the beginning of a three-year plan, the IRS will "recapture" the unpaid taxes on the payments.

FILING STATUS

How a spouse designates his or her filing status with the IRS can have an effect on the amount of taxes paid. Whether a spouse is "single" or "married" depends on the spouse's *legal* marital status on December 31 of the tax year. Therefore, if filing single will decrease a spouse's tax burden, it may be in the spouse's best interest to facilitate a divorce settlement prior to the end of the tax year. A concession made in the negotiations may be more than offset by the tax savings created by filing as a single person. The opposite may also be true. It may be in your best interest to remain married until after the end of the tax year in order to benefit from savings stemming from filing "married."

The savings will depend on each spouse's individual situation, and proposed taxes should be computed by the spouse and/ or his or her tax advisor for each of the options available.

Knowing options can speed negotiations and save both spouses on taxes and on attorney fees.

Investment decisions may have to be made regarding securities or liquid funds awarded in the divorce. It may be appropriate to engage the services of a financial advisor for this purpose. While I am aware of many of the tax consequences of divorce, I am a trial attorney and family law practitioner and NOT a tax attorney. Therefore I always recommend that every spouse obtain the services of a C.P.A. to guide him or her in making the tax decisions affecting a divorce case and property settlement, especially when a family business is involved.

CHAPTER IX
LEGAL ASPECTS OF DIVORCE

Most spouses are represented by attorneys in their divorce cases. Accordingly, this book is written with the understanding that a family law attorney represents at least one party, if not both parties.

Once you have retained a family law attorney, he or she will begin to work on your divorce. Alternative dispute resolutions, such as arbitration and mediation, are options you may want to discuss, as well as where and when to file for divorce.

STARTING THE DIVORCE

A divorce case is started by filing a Complaint for Divorce in the Circuit Court - Family Division. The complaint may be filed in the Circuit Court for the county where one spouse lives, or if separated, in the county where the other spouse lives. At least one spouse, however, must have resided in the county where the complaint for divorce is filed for at least ten days immediately before the complaint for divorce is filed. Also, at least one spouse must have lived in Michigan for at least 180 days immediately before you file. In Michigan, there is no such thing as filing jointly for divorce. One spouse must be the filing party (plaintiff) and the other is the responding party (defendant). One law firm cannot represent both spouses in the same divorce, since that would be a conflict of interest.

If a person is personally served with a divorce complaint, he or she must file an answer within 21 days. If the person is served by mail, then he or she must file an answer within 28 days or risk being defaulted. If the complaint is sent by certified mail, the postal carrier will require that the person "served" sign a receipt. If a person has been personally served (not by mail) and fails to file an answer within 21 days, he or she can be "defaulted." If defaulted, that spouse and his or her attorney will not be allowed to voice concerns at any of the hearings in the case. This could work to a party's great disadvantage when the Court decides custody, parenting time, support, and property settlement issues.

After retaining a lawyer, the lawyer should mail or email his or her client copies of all pleadings filed on the client's behalf. All clients should always be sure to review the papers that have been prepared to be filed in their cases to ensure that they say what the clients want stated. Filed court pleadings will often cause strong reactions from your spouse that will be difficult to control, so it's important that you know what's being said and when those pleadings are going to be served on your spouse or spouse's attorney. Try to be as fair as possible, and give careful consideration to the advice that you receive from your attorney.

NEGOTIATION

Dissolving a marriage requires that everyone work together so that a bad situation doesn't get worse. It is in both sides' interests to act in a civilized, courteous manner and to approach negotiations in a way that will defuse tensions, avoid hostility, and maximize the ability of the parties and their lawyers to arrive at a fair and reasonable settlement of all issues involved.

Experienced family lawyers know, and countless studies confirm, that an agreement fairly negotiated between the parties is almost always the best possible outcome, because it allows both parties to fine-tune matters that courts are ill equipped to resolve. After all, the court will never know a case as well as the parties and their lawyers. A negotiated settlement almost always costs less, is normally followed more closely by the parties, and requires fewer modifications later than a litigated one.

In a small percentage of cases, however, despite everyone's best efforts, a settlement cannot be reached. This may be due to the parties' unrealistic expectations, a dispute over the facts or the law, novel circumstances or issues, or one party's unwillingness to grant the other a divorce. It can also be caused by the other party's lawyer who either cannot control his or her client or that just gives the client bad advice. Sometimes lawyers set unreasonable goals for their clients by over selling the client on what they can "get for them."

Unless one party is in default for having refused to timely file an answer to the other party's complaint for divorce or for refusal to cooperate in the discovery process, no settlement can be reached without both parties' consultation and approval.

TEMPORARY ORDERS

Often, it is necessary to get some kind of immediate relief when the divorce is filed. It may be a restraining order, immediate temporary support, control of assets, child custody, or parenting time orders, a right to remain in the marital residence, or payment of attorney fees. In such cases, a lawyer files a motion and schedules a court hearing or requests that the judge sign an order directing the other party to appear for a court hearing to "show cause" why the court should not grant the requested relief. The hearing usually is held within a few weeks after the papers are filed and served. The temporary orders may be changed during the divorce case or when a final judgment of divorce is entered (when your case is settled or tried by a family law judge).

At temporary relief hearings, the court may take testimony or may proceed on the basis of the documents filed or the lawyers' offers of proof. Time generally is limited, and many courts prefer not to take testimony.

When a new divorce case is filed, **under exceptional circumstances**, the judge can order one party to have temporary custody of the children. This temporary order will remain in effect unless the defendant (the spouse who did not file for divorce) files a written objection and requests a hearing within 14 days after being served with the complaint and court's temporary orders. If a hearing is requested, the judge can change the custody pending a recommendation from a Friend of the Court Referee hearing or the parties' final settlement or trial. Because a party has only 14 days to object to a temporary order, and only 21 or 28 days to file an answer (depending on how the party was served), a party should contact an experienced family law attorney as soon as possible after he or she has been served with legal documents.

TEMPORARY SUPPORT

Support needs, for children and/or one of the divorcing spouses, are some of the most common reasons for an immediate hearing. By local court rule, such temporary support hearings usually take place before a Friend of the Court Referee. At such a hearing, the party seeking support will present evidence of his or her needs, obligations, expenses, and income. The spouse from whom support is sought will also be given an opportunity to present evidence of his or her expenses, debts, and income. The temporary support set at this first hearing is important to both parties. Temporary orders are usually in effect through the completion of trial.

A party may ask the court to rule on other issues, such as who should remain in the family home during the divorce proceeding, who will control certain assets (such as a car), and who is responsible for certain debts.

MODIFYING TEMPORARY ORDERS

Often there will be a need to adjust custody, parenting time, support, temporary alimony, or other arrangements during the divorce case. This is done by one party's attorney filing a motion with the court and scheduling a hearing where both attorneys can state the views of their clients. These hearings are usually very short and usually only the attorneys speak to the judge. Spouses not represented by an attorney will be allowed to speak for themselves.

UNCONTESTED CASES

In a default or uncontested case, only one party needs to go to court. A responding party defaults if he or she fails to answer the complaint within the allotted time. A divorce is uncontested if the parties reach a compromise on every issue. In either case, the actual court appearance will be short. Testimony is needed to prove that grounds for divorce exist. Such testimony is what is referred to as putting the "proofs on the record." After hearing such testimony, and whatever the parties have agreed to regarding property settlement, alimony, and child custody matters, the judge will then grant a judgment of the dissolution of the parties' marriage.

CONTESTED CASES

If it seems unlikely that a client's case will settle, or if a client's lawyer determines that having a trial date might encourage settlement, he or she will request a trial date. The court may also schedule trial, usually after a final pretrial hearing or conference is conducted.

DISCOVERY

Once the case has been started and an answer or default filed, the process of "discovery" begins. This process allows each spouse to "discover" what property, income, or other information is in the possession of the other spouse. Michigan law provides for "liberal" discovery. This means that both spouses are required to turn over nearly every type of information about themselves (medical, emotional, financial) to their spouse's attorneys upon request.

The actual discovery procedures may be as informal as a telephone call from one spouse's lawyer requesting any checking account records the other spouse has, or as formal as a long list of questions the client will be required to answer under oath (interrogatories).

In most family law cases, both spouses will be asked to produce documents and records and respond to questions. It is essential that both sides have all the information and documentation necessary to prepare for trial and to form the basis for meaningful settlement discussions.

By approaching these matters, in the spirit of cooperation, each spouse reduces the time required for discovery and the cost of the case. Many lawyers try to gather as much information as possible informally. When this informal approach is inadequate, however, a client's lawyer must resort to the procedures provided under Michigan law in adversary proceeding. Some of these procedures include:

1. **Admissions:** A spouse may be required to admit or deny facts set forth in certain specific written statements. These require immediate attention because by law, a response must be received within a specified time; for example, if a party does not respond within 28 days to a request for admissions submitted by his or her spouse, **they are deemed admitted** and the court accepts such admissions as facts.

2. **Interrogatories:** Each spouse may submit a list of detailed written questions. These must be answered (under oath) within the allotted time. **If the other spouse fails to respond within the time required, he or she may be compelled by the court to answer or may be fined, be declared to be "in default," or have his or her case dismissed.**

3. **Depositions:** In its simplest form, a discovery deposition is the oral testimony of a witness taken under oath before trial. Most of the evidentiary objections available at trial do not apply

at a discovery deposition. Questions must focus exclusively on relevant case information.

4. Other forms of discovery are:

Requests for Production of Documents, Requests for Entry onto Land, Request for Vocational Evaluations, and Requests for Physical or Psychological Evaluations.

DEPOSITIONS

A party's deposition (or a witness' deposition) may be taken during the divorce action. A deposition is an important procedure for which a client and his or her lawyer will prepare. The following instructions will help clients understand what a deposition is, why it is being taken, how it works, how they should act, and pitfalls to avoid.

PRE-DEPOSITION INSTRUCTIONS

1. What is a deposition? A deposition is the testimony of a witness taken under oath before trial in the presence of a court reporter. Opposing counsel will ask the questions and a court reporter will record the lawyer's questions and the answers of the person being deposed. The person being deposed is entitled to have his or her lawyer present, but the judge will not be present. In all likelihood, the deposition will take place in one of the lawyer's conference rooms. The testimony a client gives at a deposition will be similar to what he or she will later testify to in court should the case go to trial.

Most experienced family law attorneys have a DVD for you to view prior to testifying at a deposition or at trial. Such a DVD will help prepare you by showing you what to expect at your deposition. Hopefully, viewing such DVD will also help put you at ease, since it will help you have the confidence of being prepared for your deposition.

2. The purpose of a deposition. Opposing counsel will take a spouse's deposition for three main reasons:

a) To find out the person's personal knowledge of the facts and issues in the case; in other words, to learn his or her story and what he or she will say in court.

b) To pin a person down to a specific story so that he or she will have to tell that same version of the story in court or be open to having his or her truthfulness challenged.

c) To see if the person can be caught in a lie so as to persuade the court that such person is not a truthful person and therefore his or her testimony should not be believed on any of the points, particularly the crucial ones.

These are legitimate purposes and opposing counsel has every right to take a witness' deposition. Likewise, both spouses have the same right to take the depositions of their spouse and all possible witnesses.

3. Pitfalls to avoid. Always remember that as a litigant or witness, your only goal is to testify to the facts as you know them.

a) <u>Do not give opinions</u>. Generally speaking, if you are asked a question that calls for an opinion, your attorney may object to the question. However, if your lawyer advises you to go ahead and answer after the objection, then answer.

b) <u>Never state facts that are not known</u>. Even if you say you don't know and it makes it appear that you are ignorant or evasive, you still should not guess or estimate when giving an answer. If the answer is wrong, your spouse can use it to show that you didn't know what you were talking about or to imply that you were deliberately not telling the truth.

c) <u>Never try to explain or justify an answer</u>. Doing so might make it appear that you doubted the accuracy or authenticity of your testimony.

d) <u>Only give readily available information</u>. Do not ask your lawyer for information or ask another witness for information. Do not volunteer to look up anything or supplement an answer unless your lawyer tells you to do so.

e) <u>Do not reach into your purse, wallet, or briefcase for any documents or information unless your lawyer directs you to do so.</u> Likewise, do not ask your lawyer for any documents in your lawyer's case file.

f) **<u>Do not get angry.</u>** Anger destroys the effect of your testimony and may cause you to say things that can be used against you later in negotiations or trial.

g) <u>Do not argue with the opposing attorney.</u> Give the information you have. That is all the opposing counsel is entitled to receive. Answer questions in an ordinary tone of voice. Emotional responses to certain matters could give your spouse an advantage. That being said, if you are sad and tears are natural, be yourself. You are human and no apology is necessary.

h) <u>If your attorney starts to speak, **stop answering immediately,** and allow your attorney to talk.</u> If your attorney is objecting to the question, do not speak until he or she advises you to answer or the opposing counsel asks the next question.

i) <u>Take your time</u>. The transcript of your deposition does not show how long it takes you to answer. Think about each question and answer it in a straightforward manner.

j) <u>Tell the truth</u>. The truth will never hurt. Your attorney may be able to explain away the truth, but your attorney cannot explain away a lie or a concealment of the truth.

k) <u>Never joke in a deposition</u>. Humor will not be apparent on the transcript and will make you look crude or cavalier about telling the truth.

l) <u>Do not volunteer facts</u>. Simply answer the exact question asked, yes or no. Do not elaborate unless asked to do so. Such "additional" information volunteered by you may hinder your case.

m) <u>After the deposition, do not chat with your spouse or your spouse's lawyer</u>. Remember, during the divorce process, your spouse and his or her attorney are your legal adversaries. Do not let good manners cause you to drop your guard.

n) <u>If you do not understand the question asked, request that the question be rephrased or repeated</u>. Make a statement such as, "Could you please rephrase the question so I can be sure what you're asking before I respond as I want to make sure my answer is accurate?" Additionally, don't anticipate questions. Make sure to understand the questions before you respond.

MEDIATION

Once discovery is completed, a settlement can be negotiated. If the parties are unable to reach an agreement, they may decide to hire a mediator to assist them. In some cases, the court will order that a mediator be used. If ordered by the court, the mediator will be an experienced family law attorney, counselor, or court personnel. If selected by the parties, the mediator could be a lawyer, social worker, accountant, or anybody the parties believe can assist them in settling their case. Mediation is typically very successful in settling divorce cases.

GOING TO TRIAL

If you can't reach a settlement through negotiation or mediation, the divorce case will go to trial. Absent a unique tort claim, there are no jury trials in divorce cases. Some judges do not "like to hear" divorce trials because they often present difficult emotional issues. For that and other reasons, such as crowded dockets, several scheduled trial dates may come and go without an actual trial taking place. The amount of delay varies from county to county. These delays often give the parties an additional opportunity to reach a settlement. They can also pressure parties, anxious to end the marriage, into reaching a settlement (which often they later regret having done). Accordingly, listen to the advice of your attorney, and if necessary, be patient and allow the process to be completed.

YOUR DAY IN COURT

Going to court is bound to raise your anxiety. Knowing what is going to happen and how to act helps diminish your nervousness. Also, keep in mind that the family law attorney, if experienced, will be very familiar with what helps the trier of fact (the judge in divorce cases) make up his or her mind on crucial issues. Together, he or she will assist the court to make the best decision possible for a party and any affected minor children, as the case may be.

Tell the truth. Don't guess. Be sure to understand each question, and answer only that question. As with depositions, do not volunteer information when testifying in court. For example, if you are asked how many children are in your family, simply give the number. Do not volunteer additional information such as "We have two children. I wanted more, but because I spent five years in prison, we were unable to have a larger family."

1. **Take your time and talk loudly enough for everyone to hear.** Don't chew gum, and keep your hands away from your mouth.

2. **Be courteous.** Don't argue with the other lawyer and do not lose your temper.

3. **Don't be afraid.** Look at the person who asks the questions and be as positive as you can. Just tell your story, in your own words, to the best of your ability.

4. **Be sincere and direct.** Keep to the point.

5. **Do not be ashamed to tell the whole story.** This is your one day in court. The outcome of the case may well depend on the facts that you and your witnesses disclose.

Your lawyer will consult with you during the course of the trial. As the trial progresses, tell your lawyer, by passing a note or by a whisper, anything that you believe he or she should know. Be careful, however, not to distract your lawyer. Particularly during testimony, your lawyer must concentrate totally on each question and answer, as well as the reactions of the judge and opposing counsel, and be ready to object instantly to improper questions.

If a party's case goes to trial, the judge decides all issues involved in a contested divorce case. The judge listens to the testimony, weighs the evidence, determines facts and the equities (fairness), and applies the law as he/she sees fit. **Currently, case law calls for ten factors to be considered by the court in making a property settlement. They are:**

1. age of the parties;
2. health of the parties;
3. sources of the property;
4. length of the marriage;
5. how the property was accumulated;
6. needs of the parties;

7. needs of any minor children;

8. earning ability and capacity of the parties;

9. **fault of the parties***;

10. other equitable factors.

The property to be divided can include common items such as a house, cars, and bank accounts. The property to be divided can also include professional degrees and practices, businesses, pensions, profit-sharing plans and other assets not normally thought of as property. Although every judge views property division differently, the most common approach is to divide the property equally between the husband and wife (absent "fault").

*If one spouse has physically abused the other spouse, or committed an act of adultery that led to the breakdown of the parties' marriage, the court may use such fault of the offending spouse to change the property spilt from 50/50 to 55/45 or possibly 60/40.

<u>Alimony</u> may be ordered by the court in addition to dividing the parties' assets. Alimony is paid by one spouse to the other for his/her support. **Currently, based on case law, the court considers 14 factors when determining whether to award alimony. The 14 factors are:**

1. the past relations and conduct of the parties;

2. the length of the marriage;

3. the abilities of the parties to work;

4. the source and amount of property awarded to the parties;

5. the parties' ages;

6. the abilities of the parties to pay alimony;

7. the present situation of the parties;

8. the needs of the parties;

9. the parties' health;

10. the prior standard of living of the parties and whether either is responsible for the support of others;

11. contributions of the parties to the joint estate;

12. a party's fault in causing the divorce;

13. the effect of cohabitation on a party's financial status; and

14. general principles of equity.

Alimony can be permanent (until the recipient's death or remarriage) or rehabilitative. Rehabilitative alimony is designed to provide support for a few years while the recipient receives job training or completes an education. Rehabilitative alimony is also referred to as transitional alimony. Alimony is usually taxable to the recipient and deductible by the payor.

If a divorce judgment is silent on the issue of alimony, alimony is reserved and may be reopened at any time after entry of the judgment of divorce. Alimony is usually modifiable at any time upon a showing of changed circumstances. Alimony may be raised, lowered, or canceled depending on: (a) the ability of the payor to pay; and (b) the need of the party who is receiving the alimony (the payee). Modification of alimony granted in a divorce judgment must be based upon changed circumstances that take place following entry of the divorce judgment. By agreement of the parties, alimony can also be made non-modifiable. Making alimony non-modifiable can be risky to both parties and good legal advice is needed before making such a decision.

Alimony (also referred to as spousal support) is alive and well in Michigan. Depending on the attitude of the family law judge assigned to your case, it is either available to help a spouse "adjust to being divorced" or to support a divorced spouse in a style he or she was accustomed to during the marriage.

A 20- to 30-year marriage, where the wife stayed at home to raise the parties' children while her husband worked long hours to build a business into a profitable enterprise, often results in a large award of long-term or permanent alimony. This is especially true if the husband has found a new lady to spend his "free time" with and such an offense was the fault that led to ending the marriage.

SETTLING YOUR CASE

Even if the case is settled, a divorce cannot be granted without a court hearing. At that hearing, one of the parties (usually the spouse who filed the divorce complaint) will testify that the statements made in the complaint (or counter-claim) are true, and that there has been a "breakdown in the marriage relationship to the extent that the objects of matrimony have been destroyed and that there remains no reasonable likelihood that the marriage may be preserved." The terms of the settlement will also be placed on the court's record. Such a hearing typically lasts 10 to 30 minutes.

DIVORCE JUDGMENT

The document that ends a divorce case and grants the divorce is called a divorce judgment. It contains the property settlement of the parties, the custody, parenting time, child support, and alimony terms agreed to by the parties or as ordered by the court. The parties' divorce is not final until the divorce judgment is signed by the judge and the signed judgment is actually filed with the court clerk. This may not happen for days or weeks after the judge has granted the divorce in open court.

Except for fraud, or in an extremely unusual case, a party cannot appeal a divorce judgment that he or she agreed to, in writing or in open court. If a party's case was tried by the court, a party has an automatic right to appeal the court's ruling to the Michigan Court of Appeals. The party must file his or her claim of appeal within 21 days after the judgment is signed by the judge and filed with the court's clerk.

Under Michigan law, divorced parents with minor children (or parents in the process of a divorce) typically cannot move the domicile (residence) of the parties' minor children from the State of Michigan or more than 100 miles from the children's legal residence at the time of the commencement of the divorce action, without the prior approval of the court. Michigan divorce judgments normally contain this language unless some other agreement was reached by the parties with the approval of the court. If *both* parties consent to a child's domicile being moved more than 100 miles or from the State of Michigan, the court still technically needs to determine that such a move is in the best interest of the parties' minor children. That being said, the court will almost always agree to an order that has been stipulated to by both parties, especially if both parties are represented by counsel.

CHAPTER X

FRIEND OF THE COURT

As previously stated, the Friend of the Court is an individual appointed by the chief judge for the Circuit Court of each county. That being said, staff being supervised by the Friend of the Court are often referred to by parties as the "FOC." In such regard, the Friend of the Court is often viewed as a staff of people who collectively assist parties in resolving child custody, parenting time, and child support issues. Typically, in most counties, staff from the Friend of the Court's office also make recommendations regarding spousal support.

FAQS REGARDING THE FOC:

WHO IS THE FRIEND OF THE COURT?

The Friend of the Court is an agency of the Circuit Court established by the Michigan Legislature to assist the Circuit

Court in divorce and related cases. Each county Circuit Court has a Friend of the Court office and staff to assist parties in family law cases and more specifically to assist the family law judge(s). The office typically employs lawyers, social workers, administrators, accountants, and other professionals.

WHAT DOES THE FRIEND OF THE COURT DO?

Collection and Disbursement of Support

The Friend of the Court is perhaps best known as the agency that initiates collection and disbursement of child support payments. This is now done in conjunction with the Michigan State Disbursement Unit (MiSDU) in Lansing. When a support payor falls behind in payments, the Friend of the Court will initiate enforcement proceedings.

Investigation and Recommendation

The Friend of the Court also investigates and makes recommendations concerning child support, alimony, custody, and parenting time. In most counties, a lawyer employed by the Friend of the Court, called a referee, will conduct hearings on one or more of these issues and issue a recommended order to the Circuit Court. Many Circuit judges will require that the case first be investigated by the Friend of the Court, or in some cases heard by a Friend of the Court Referee, before a judicial hearing will be granted.

Mediation

Staff of the Friend of the Court Office also typically offer mediation services to help resolve custody, parenting time, or support disputes.

Specifics

Parties to a divorce will receive a Friend of the Court handbook at the beginning of the divorce process, which spells out each county's unique policies for dealing with child custody/parenting time issues. This handbook also describes the process whereby parties can request the assistance of the Friend of the Court personnel to resolve issues with their spouses during the divorce process and, more importantly, after the divorce has been finalized with the judgment of divorce. These services are usually helpful to the parties and can save the parties untold legal expenses by utilizing such services rather than litigating issues down the road.

Opting Out

While I typically recommend that most parties **not** opt-out of the Friend of the Court services, since many of these services will be helpful to them in the future, sometimes parties want to resolve everything between themselves and have the court not involved as much as possible. If such is the case, the parties do not have to use the services of the Friend of the Court.

They will have to file a motion to "opt-out" and the motion will usually then be granted by the court. Prior to entry of the court's order, however, the parties must file a document that includes a list of the Friend of the Court services and sign an acknowledgment that the parties are choosing to opt out of having those services provided by the Friend of the Court. The opt-out motion must be timely filed, typically at the same time as the complaint for divorce is filed, or shortly thereafter. If timely filed, the court must order the Friend of the Court not to open a case unless one of more of the following is true:

a) The party is eligible for the Title IV-D of the Social Security Act 42 U.S.C. Section 601, et sic (child support services) because the parties are receiving or have applied for public assistance;

b) The party has applied for IV-D services;

c) A party has requested the Friend of the Court to open a case; or

d) There is evidence of domestic violence or uneven bargaining positions, and request is against the best interest of the parties or the parties' minor child(ren).

The parties may also file a motion requesting the court to order the Friend of the Court to close its case. The court will issue the order unless it determines one of the following:

a) A party objects to the closure;

b) A party is receiving public assistance;

c) Within the previous 12 months, an arrearage or custody/parenting time violation has occurred in the case;

d) Within the previous 12 months, a party to the case has reopened the Friend of the Court case (parties can opt-out of the Friend of the Court services only once); or

e) There is evidence of domestic violence or uneven bargaining positions and the request is against the best interest of the parties or the parties' minor child(ren).

Closing a Friend of the Court case requires the parties to assume full responsibility for administrating and enforcing the court's order. Nevertheless, to assure proper accounting of support payments, the parties may choose to have support payments made through MISDU even after the Friend of the Court case is closed [MCL 552.505a(6)]. A party may reopen a Friend of the Court case by applying for public assistance or requesting services from the Friend of the Court.

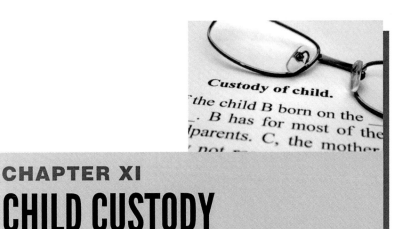

CHAPTER XI
CHILD CUSTODY

When there are minor children and the divorcing parents cannot agree on custody, parenting time, or child support, the final decision on these issues is made by the family law judge hearing the divorce case. Custody is one of the most emotional and traumatic issues in any divorce case.

CUSTODY OPTIONS

Custody options include sole legal custody or joint legal custody, and sole physical custody or joint physical custody. The parties may choose to share custody with one parent having a certain number of overnights and the other parent (or a third party) having the remainder. The basis for determining child custody is the "best interests of the child." Due to the complex nature of custody disputes, this subject is best left to an in-depth discussion when you visit with an experienced family law attorney.

LEGAL CUSTODY

Legal custody means decision-making authority for the important decisions that affect the minor child or children. Such decisions include where the child or children attend school, go to

church, and what activities they are allowed to participate in during their minority. Medical care decisions and decisions regarding whether a 16- or 17-year-old can marry are also such important decisions that affect the minor child or children. The court favors both parties sharing legal custody (although there is no statutory presumption in favor of joint legal custody). If the court orders that one parent have sole legal custody, the court must state on the record why it is not ordering joint legal custody, e.g., the parties typically cannot agree on important decisions. An award of joint legal custody (joint decision-making) may accompany an order granting sole physical custody (where the child primarily resides) to only one of the parents. The other parent is entitled to parenting time with the child or children, but is referred to as the noncustodial parent.

Whether a parent has legal custody also affects whether the other parent is bound by Michigan's 100-mile prohibition of moving (with the minor child or children) without first obtaining approval of the other parent and/or the court. If one parent has sole legal and sole physical custody, then such parent can move away from the other parent any distance within the state of Michigan without first obtaining approval from the other parent or the court. On the other hand, if both parties share joint legal custody (or physical custody), then agreement of the parties is required, or if both parties cannot agree, then the court decides the issue. When the court decides the issue, the court balances the needs of the spouse wanting to move and the children's best interests, and how such a move would affect the relationship between the minor children (going with the moving spouse) and the other parent.

PHYSICAL CUSTODY

Physical custody is defined as where the minor children spend their nights. When the children spend 183 or more overnights with one parent, as opposed to the other, then the parent with the most overnights *can* be viewed as "the custodial parent." In most cases, however, if the overnights are close, 190 or 200 to one parent, the parties will describe their physical custody arrangement as joint physical. The overnight pattern is usually one pattern during the school year and another pattern for the summer for school-aged children. A typical school year custody arrangement might be every Sunday through Thursday night with the custodial parent and every other Friday and Saturday night with the non-custodial parent. This 12/2 parenting schedule would switch to half of the summer or more for the non-custodial parent during the summer break from school. Other options include a 7/7 parenting time schedule year round or 8/6 parenting time year round. The parties can also agree to a 9/5 or 10/4 parenting time schedule that rotates every 14 days during the school year and then switches to a 7/7 parenting time schedule during the summer.

CHANGING THE CHILDREN'S SCHOOLING

If both parents share legal or physical custody (such that one parent would have more than an every-other-weekend overnight parenting time arrangement), the other parent may be able to prevent the change in the child's or children's school if he or she has not agreed that such a change of schools is best for the child or children.

Even a change in schools in the same area can be a basis for requiring a court's decision if the parties share custody (legal or physical), if such a change will affect the children's "established custodial environment" or the parent sharing legal custody does not agree to a change in schools (e.g., from one elementary school to another), from home schooling to a public school, or from a private school or parochial school to a public school (and vice versa). Spouses who believe they may be relocating their residence, for whatever reason (e.g., a new job or a new relationship) should, if at all possible, carefully negotiate the issue of legal custody and parenting time during the divorce process to make such a move possible in the future without having to return to court. Having good legal advice in such regard can save a spouse thousands of dollars in legal expenses and untold grief in the future by negotiating these issues up front during the divorce proceeding. Being able to relocate, especially out of state, after a judgment of divorce is entered, may not be possible without the party wishing to move having to leave minor children behind with the other parent, who would more likely than not become the primary custodial parent of the children.

CHILD CUSTODY ACT

A parent involved in a child custody matter should become acquainted with the "Child Custody Act," which sets forth 12 factors that a judge must consider when making a custody decision. Those factors are:

a) the love, affection, and other emotional ties existing between the parties involved and the child;

b) the capacity and disposition of the parties involved to give the child love, affection, and guidance, and continuation of the educating and raising of the child and its religion or creed, if any;

c) the capacity and disposition of the parties involved to provide the child with food, clothing, medical care or other remedial care, recognized and permitted under the laws of this state in place of medical care, and other material needs;

d) the length of time the child has lived in a stable, satisfactory environment, and the desirability of maintaining continuity;

e) the permanence, as a family unit, of the existing or proposed custodial home or homes;

f) the moral fitness of the parties involved;

g) the mental and physical health of the parties involved;

h) the home, school, and community record of the child;

i) the reasonable preference of the child, if the court deems the child to be of sufficient age to express preference;

j) the willingness and ability of each of the parents to facilitate and encourage a close and continuing parent-child relationship between the child and the other parent;

k) domestic violence; and

l) any other factors considered by the court to be relevant to a particular child custody dispute.

CHAPTER XII
CHILD SUPPORT

Child support is money paid by one parent to the other parent for the support of the minor child or children. It can also include money for a portion of child care costs when the situation warrants. A percentage of uncovered medical expenses (co-pays, etc.) can also be ordered based on the disparity of the parties' incomes. In determining the amount of child support, Michigan has adopted a statewide child support formula, which is used to determine the normal amount of child support that will be ordered by the family court judge. Under a new federal law, the judge and the Friend of the Court must use the formula in setting support levels unless it would be grossly unfair to do so. The formula considers the incomes of both parents and the needs of the child(ren) based on state and national statistics showing what it costs to raise a child in a typical family of a similar income level.

<u>Child support should be discussed in detail with a spouse's family lawyer or a member of his or her staff, after full disclosure of both parents' finances has been made</u>. An experienced family law attorney may be able to help one of the parties pay less child support than what the formula would call for if that party makes concessions to the other spouse regarding property settlement (e.g. provides a home for the parties' minor children). Additionally, paying less child support and more in spousal support may have tax savings that the parties can both utilize considering the situation where one party is employed and the other is not. Child support is not tax deductible to the parent who is paying it, and it is not taxable to the parent who receives it.

Child support is modifiable upon a showing of "changed circumstances." Support is usually ordered until the minor child reaches the age of 18 or up to 19 1/2 if the child is still living with the custodial parent and in high school taking sufficient classes to graduate. In exceptional circumstances (such as a child having a severe physical or mental disability), support may be continued beyond the age of 18 even though the child is not attending high school.

In some cases, payment of the cost of a college education is negotiated as part of the final divorce settlement. However, absent an agreement between the parents, the court cannot order payment for college expenses. Once an agreement is made, however, it can be enforced by the court through its contempt powers.

If there is an arrearage (past due support) in child support payments, medical expenses, etc., under a temporary order (while the judgment of divorce is pending), the judgment of divorce **must** contain a provision preserving this arrearage. If temporary arrearages are not specifically preserved in the divorce judgment, they are waived (eliminated).

Automatic income withholding (wage garnishment) provisions are usually included in each temporary support order and in the support clause of the divorce judgment. This requires the non-custodial parent's employer (or other source of income) to withhold from his/her paycheck monies owing for child support. In special circumstances, the parties can agree to allow for the direct payment of child support by the payor to the payee without requiring an income withholding order. In such a case, the court must make a finding on the record pursuant to a written agreement between the parties that it is in the best interest of the minor child(ren) not to order an income withholding order for the payment of child support for specific reasons.

Other enforcement methods include interception of tax refunds, placing liens on the non-custodial parent's property, notification to credit bureaus of past-due support, and holding the non-custodial parent in contempt of court, which could result in a fine, jail, or both. Michigan courts also may allow the custodial parent to reduce outstanding support arrearages to a money judgment and to receive "interest" on the unpaid child support money owed.

Child support should be paid through the offices of the county Friend of the Court in conjunction with the Michigan State Disbursement Unit (MiSDU). This allows for accurate record keeping and prompt and inexpensive enforcement if an arrearage accrues. If direct support payments are made, record keeping and enforcement are made difficult.

If a non-custodial parent is denied parenting time, it is not the right of such parent to stop making child support payments. Support and parenting time are separate issues and should not be played against one another. If parenting time is denied contrary to court order, or if child support is not paid contrary to a court order, the court will enforce either on behalf of the aggrieved party. Non-custodial parents should not take "the law into their own hands" and withhold child support because they have been denied parenting time. Conversely, a custodial parent should not deny parenting time for the failure to receive child support. Remember, it's about the children...and their right to see both their mother and father.

Child support obligations are **not** dischargeable in bankruptcy, and are given priority over all other debts except federal income tax liens.

CHAPTER XIII
PARENTING TIME

Parenting time is the time that a parent has with a child. This is important time! It should be used to preserve and develop the relationship between parent and child. Studies have shown that the quality of the parenting time is more important than the quantity.

A law that took effect in March of 1989 strengthens a non-custodial parent's right to continued involvement in his/her child's life. That right can be denied only in the most extreme cases of harm to the child. Many non-custodial parents have "reasonable" or "reasonable and liberal" parenting time rights. This leaves the parents to jointly determine what "reasonable" and/or "liberal" parenting time means. The other alternative available upon the request of either parent is to have a specific parenting time order, which sets the times and days for the parenting time between the child and the non-custodial parent. Either provision may be included in the divorce judgment or added through a post-judgment modification.

If one parent violates the parenting time order and refuses to allow contact between the other parent and the child, the aggrieved parent should first notify the Friend of the Court in writing of the alleged parenting time denial. The Friend of the Court will make a written determination regarding whether parenting time was wrongfully denied and make a recommendation, which may include specific make-up parenting time. In some cases, the Friend of the Court may determine that the matter should be heard by the judge.

If a divorce or a custody action has been commenced or a death of a spouse has occurred, Michigan law allows **grandparents**, and in some cases, other third parties, to file a petition with the court seeking their own visitation rights with minor children— or even to seek custody.

If the Friend of the Court is unable to provide assistance, the aggrieved parent may hire an attorney to seek a contempt finding against the custodial parent in court. If the judge finds that one parent has violated the parenting time order, the court may order make-up parenting time, modify the custody or parenting time order, impose a fine or jail term, or all of the above.

When parenting time is agreed to by the parties or ordered by the court, such parenting time is typically ordered in rotations of 14 days. In such regard, the custodial parent will have the child or children spend overnights with him/her either 7, 8, 9, 10, 11, 12, or in some cases all 14 days. If one parent has the child or children with him or her for all 14 days of a two-week rotation, then the court has either found that the other parent "has issues" or is unfit. In such situations, the court may require that the parenting time be supervised, or in some cases eliminated. While supervised and no parenting time orders are rare, they are ordered if the court believes they are in the best interests of the parties' minor children. Such supervised or non-parenting time order would only be issued if the non-custodial parent was found to pose either a physical or emotional threat to the well-being of the parties' minor child or children.

Typical parenting time arrangements include one parent being the custodial parent and having the children the majority of time throughout the year. Typically, as children enter school-age years, parenting times revolve around the school year. Currently, in Michigan, school typically starts the first day after the Labor Day weekend and ends in June of the following year.

Accordingly, a 14-day rotation involving the school year typically starts in September and ends in June. During the school year, one parent may have the children from Sunday through Thursday night and the other parent may have the children from Friday night through Sunday night. When one parent is the primary custodial parent, this could result in a 12/2 parenting schedule. The non-custodial parent would have the children spend their overnights with him or her every other weekend from Friday night after school or at 6 p.m. through Sunday night at some appointed time, 5 p.m. or 6 p.m. The other parent would then have the children during the school week and the following weekend as well. During the week, it is common for the non-custodial parent to have parenting time of 2-3 hours during the week on either Tuesday or Wednesday evenings, or as the parties agree.

In recent times, more overnights tend to be allocated to the non-custodial parent such that the overnight parenting times are often some other number, such as a 11/3, 10/4, 9/5, or 8/6. Any of these combinations can result in the parties agreeing to jointly share physical custody, such that one parent might have nine overnights, while the other parent has five, and still call this parenting time arrangement a joint custody arrangement.

While these parenting times rotate every 14 days throughout the school year, additional specific holiday parenting time is dictated by the individual county. The parties typically split Thanksgiving, Christmas break, and spring break. Other holidays are recognized, as well, such as Memorial Day weekend, 4th of July, and Labor Day weekend. Some counties include Halloween and the child(ren)'s birthdays. Typically, the mother will have parenting time on Mother's Day and the father will have parenting time on Father's Day. Each county's Friend of the Court policies are published and are accessible to the parties to utilize in planning such parenting time schedules.

It is important to know that while these policies are general, parties are always encouraged to agree to whatever works best for them and their children. Parties can modify how they divide parenting time as they see fit in most cases. I often encourage the parties to have a "loosey goosey" arrangement, as that is the best parenting time arrangement for parties who seek a joint custodial parenting arrangement. Each parent should be as flexible as possible with his or her spouse in accommodating unique circumstances of either the spouse or their children. If parties can focus on what is best for the children, everybody ends up winning.

Often, the children's activities will come into play, as well as the parents' activities. If a parent's work schedule changes, and it would affect his/her parenting time with the child(ren), then both spouses should try "to make it happen" by altering the parenting schedule so that the children will have quality time with both parents. Additionally, I encourage spouses to look at the child(ren)'s parenting time with the other parent as a break, because raising children is difficult and any time the child(ren) spend time with one spouse affords the other parent time to do other things (spend time with friends or develop new relationships).

TIPS FOR BETTER PARENTING

Suggested guidelines for parents after divorce:

1. Put your children's welfare ahead of your conflict with your former spouse. Avoid involving your children in any conflict with your former spouse.

2. Remember that children need two parents. Help your children maintain a positive relationship with their other parent; give them permission to love that parent.

3. <u>Show respect for the other parent.</u> Do not make derogatory remarks to or in front of the children.

4. <u>Honor your time-sharing schedule.</u> Always notify the other parent if you will be late or cannot spend time with the children. Children may view missed visits, especially without notification, as rejection.

5. <u>If you are the non-custodial parent, do not fill every minute with special activities.</u> They need at-home-time with you.

6. <u>Do not use the children as messengers or spies.</u> DO NOT pump them for information about the other parent.

7. <u>Strive for agreement on major decisions about your child's welfare and discipline so that you are not undermining the other parent.</u>

8. <u>Use common sense in exercising your custodial and parenting time rights.</u> Follow the old adage, "Do not make a mountain out of a molehill" and follow the Golden Rule: "Do unto others as you would have them do unto you."

9. Don't send or collect child support through the children.

CHAPTER XIV

CUSTODY/PARENTING TIME FOR THIRD PARTIES/GRANDPARENTS

Whenever a husband or a wife files an action for divorce, and minor children are involved, **it is possible** that a third person may bring an action for custody of such couple's child or children (under certain limited instances which are set forth in Michigan statutes). A guardian or limited guardian may also have standing to bring a custody action.

The case where such intervention might occur is when minor children have been placed with a grandparent, brother or sister, or even a close friend, and the parents have basically abdicated their responsibility as parents. If a custodial environment "becomes established," where children are essentially being raised by neither parent and the parents begin an action for divorce, then the third party who has "standing" to file a petition to intervene may do so and ask the court to award custody of the minor child or children to the third party.

Even in such a case, there is a parental presumption in favor of parents that has been adopted by the legislature. Additionally, the presumption in favor of parents being awarded custody of their children is superior to the presumption of not breaking up an established custodial environment with a child or children with a third party.

Accordingly, a third party seeking custody, as opposed to a natural parent, would have to show by clear and convincing evidence that the child or children would be better off with custody being awarded to the third party. Such an analysis would be performed under Michigan's best interests factors as set forth by Michigan statute.

I have represented several grandparents who have filed petitions to intervene and gain custody, **as opposed to grandparenting time**. In order to do so, it is generally necessary to show that both parents are unfit to raise their children. However, it might still be possible to demonstrate that one or both parents, though fit to parent, have voluntarily chosen to abdicate their parenting responsibilities for years and given deference to a third party raising their children.

With permission of my clients, I relate the following two cases. In the first case, I represented a wonderful grandmother who sought custody of her son's three minor children (her grandchildren) upon the death of her son. The mother of the children had an addiction issue with cocaine. Although the court allowed the mother time to rehabilitate herself, eventually the guardian who was caring for the children sought custody, thereby allowing the grandmother to petition to intervene in that case.

After a four-day trial, the court awarded my client custody of the three young boys. The story continues to be one where these children have been truly blessed to have their grandmother as their custodial parent. She and her husband have done a wonderful job raising her deceased son's three children, who continue to thrive in every respect. From their grandmother, I continue to receive pictures, reports of great grades in school, and stories of each child's accomplishments. This type of case allows me to sleep well at night, knowing that I may have played a small part in changing not only the lives of those three children, but the next generation that will follow as well.

In a second case, I represented a grandmother who had helped raise three grandchildren while her son and daughter-in-law had drug-related problems. After she and other family members had contacted Child Protective Services, the children were removed from their parents and made wards of the court. While the children were wards of the court, I petitioned the circuit court for a grandparenting order requesting specific court-ordered visitation with the three minor children who were now wards of the court. Initially, there was confusion as to my client's standing to request court ordered grandparenting time. The Friend of Court Referee was reluctant to conduct a grandparenting time hearing since the grandchildren had been made wards of the court due to their parents' neglect. I pointed out to court officials, however, that unless a grandparenting time order was issued, should the parents have their parental rights terminated, the grandchildren's rights to be with their paternal grandmother would be terminated as well.

One and one half years later, the Probate Court terminated the parental rights of both parents. In the interim I had secured, from the Circuit Court, a grandparenting order providing for monthly grandparenting time with the grandchildren even though the Department of Human Services (DHS) had opposed my client's request.

Contrary to doing what was in the best interest of the grandchildren, DHS had honored the request of the neglectful parents to keep their children away from the children's grandmother. As previously stated, the grandmother had been one of those persons contacting Child Protective Services about the children's parents using drugs and not watching the children. This caused the parents to be upset with her. Even though Child Protective Services encourages family members to report abuse and neglect cases, once DHS begins working with abusive or neglectful parents, DHS's goal becomes reunification of the parents and the affected children. As such, DHS honored the unfit parents' request that their children not be allowed to see the paternal grandmother, even though there was evidence that the grandmother had spent years raising the two older grandchildren and that there was a close emotional bond between the grandchildren and her.

Once the parental rights of the grandchildren's father and mother were terminated, the grandmother had her grandparenting time expanded, with an eye toward allowing her to adopt her three grandchildren. Recently, the grandmother has adopted all three children!

In both cases, had the grandmother not acted quickly, the grandchildren would have been cut out of the paternal family forever. It is often said that it takes a village to raise a child. It's also well known that families have historically raised children and grandchildren and, in many cases, the law recognizes this by allowing grandparenting time to be ordered, including grandparents actually being awarded custody of minor children.

GRANDPARENTING TIME

The statute that addresses grandparenting time is MCL 722.27b. In Michigan, a grandparent may seek grandparenting time if: (1) an action for divorce, separate maintenance, or annulment involving the child's parents is pending before the court; (2) the child's parents are divorced, separated under a judgment of separate maintenance, or have had their marriage annulled; (3) the child's parent, who was the child of the grandparents, is deceased; (4) the child's parents have never been married, they are not residing in the same household, and paternity has been established; (5) legal custody of the child has been given to a person other than the child's parent or the child is placed outside of and does not reside in the home of a parent; or (6) in the year proceeding the commencement of the action for grandparenting time, the grandparent provided an established custodial environment for the child, whether or not the grandparent had custody under a court order.

Most jurists refer to the rights of a grandparent to have grand-parenting time as a right held by the grandparent. I prefer referring to this as a right held by the grandchildren, to-wit: a right of the grandchild to see his or her grandmother and/or grandfather, based on an emotional bond that exists between the grandchild and the grandparent(s).

As a condition precedent to seeking grandparenting time, there must be "a denial" of grandparenting time by the person having custody of the grandchild. Typically, this is a surviving parent when the other parent has died. There may be ill will or bad feelings between the surviving parent and the grandparents and the grandparents feel cut off from their grandchild(ren). In order for grandparents to be successful in pursuing grandpar-enting time with their grandchild(ren), they will need proof that a close emotional bond has existed between the grandparent(s) and the grandchild(ren).

There will be times, for whatever reason, when a divorcing party may know that after divorce he or she intends to spend little time with his or her child. In such event, consideration could be given to include the grandparents in the party's custody order. A perfectly good example of this could be when parties are divorcing and the father or mother may be going overseas to serve in the military for an extended time. While there is a statute that comes into play (granting family members of the armed forces the right to exercise the parent-ing rights of the armed forces spouse), the parties may never-theless be better off by providing in their judgment of divorce that the parenting time that was to be exercised by the spouse in the military is to be exercised by designated by members of the military spouse's family.

This can also be the case in a non-military situation where one of the parties will be moving to another state or just isn't interested in spending much time with his or her own children. The children may be very bonded with their grandparents, and such facts can be taken into consideration when the couple is divorcing.

TIP: It is the better practice to spell out in the judgment of divorce, the rights of the parties' children to be with their grandparents or other third parties. After divorce, "things change" and "understandings" may become forgotten.

CHAPTER XV
DOMESTIC VIOLENCE

If spouses are victims of domestic violence, they need to first realize that they are not alone. Domestic violence is defined as physical and/or mental mistreatment of a spouse or live-in mate. As many as one-third of our nation's homes experience domestic violence. Some studies indicate that two-thirds of all marriages have experienced domestic violence.

Domestic violence is learned behavior. A large percentage of abusive male spouses were beaten as children or witnessed their mothers being abused. Although much more rare, women can also be abusers of men or children. If families are to break the cycle of domestic violence, this problem cannot be ignored and treatment must be sought.

All persons have the right to be free from fear and violence. Be sure to tell your family law attorney if you have been abused, so court protection can be sought for you.

CIVIL COMPLAINT

Although not often pursued, Michigan law does allow one spouse to sue the other for civil damages. Accordingly, if one spouse commits an intentional tort (e.g., assault and battery), the injured party can sue the spouse for committing the civil wrong. Any monetary damages could be "settled" within the divorce action as part of the property settlement.

CRIMINAL COMPLAINT

Any unwanted touching (a battery) or causing fear of physical injury (an assault) is a criminal act. Michigan criminal laws provide for an immediate arrest of an abuser if that person assaults or batters a spouse or former spouse. A spouse can also file a civil suit against a spouse and potentially collect monetary damages for the wrong, or the "tort" that the spouse committed against her or him.

Prosecutors are not always able to follow through with criminal charges in domestic assault cases. Many victims are unwilling to testify against the assailant. This unwillingness stems from the complex emotional and financial dynamics of the relationship and cannot be "blamed" on the victim. However, if criminal charges are pursued, the victim can request that the assailant be ordered to have no contact with the victim as a condition of the assailant's bond (money paid or conditions imposed in exchange for release from jail pending trial). If bond is granted to the assailant and contact is made with the victim, the bond can be revoked by the judge, and the assailant can be jailed pending trial or rehearing on the bond.

If a person has difficulty filing criminal charges, seek assistance from a local domestic violence agency or its attorney. Many of these agencies have a good working relationship with law enforcement officials. They may be very helpful in pursuing criminal charges.

ABUSE INJUNCTIONS/PERSONAL PROTECTION ORDERS

An injunction is a court order. It prohibits a person from acting in certain ways. An abuse injunction prohibits an abusive spouse or former spouse from:

a) Assaulting, beating, molesting, or wounding the victim; and/or

b) Entering into the premises of the residence or place of employment of the victim.

A person need not file for divorce to obtain an abuse injunction. Both married and single victims of domestic violence have the right to request an injunction. They need only prove to the court, by sworn written statement (affidavit), or by testimony in court, that they are victims of domestic violence and fear further injury from the assailant.

As in all family law matters, the judge has great discretion in deciding whether to grant an injunction. Some judges will not issue an injunction for a married person unless he/she files for divorce. Many judges will not order the assailant from the home **unless the abuse is "serious"** (causing physical injury) **and recent.** When you discuss your case with your family law attorney, he or she or a domestic violence agency will help you know what to expect from the court when you make your request for an injunction.

In 1995, Michigan law was amended to create Personal Protection Orders (PPOs) that can be obtained when two parties have lived together (whether married or not) and problems between them exist wherein physical violence, harassment, or stalking is a component of the parties' relationship. The aggrieved party can now go to the clerk's office and obtain forms to file a complaint and motion for a Personal Protection Order. The request can be "Ex-Parte" (where the other party does not get a chance to be heard), if the situation is very serious, and you or your children are in immediate danger. If granted, this order will not be permanent and you will eventually have to schedule an evidentiary hearing to make the temporary Ex-Parte Order permanent before the Ex-Parte Order expires. At any hearing, the aggrieved party must appear, testify, and offer any witnesses to prove the allegations against the other party.

In either case, when the court enters an Ex-Parte Personal Protection Order, or after a hearing, the court has the power to order that the "other party" is prohibited from:

1. Entering onto the property where the aggrieved person(s) lives or works;

2. Entering into some other property frequented by the aggrieved party (e.g., her mother's residence, his friend's residence);

3. Assaulting, attacking, beating, molesting, or wounding the petitioner or the petitioner's child(ren);

4. Removing the aggrieved person's minor child(ren);

5. Harassing or stalking the aggrieved party, including engaging in a number of prohibited acts (e.g., sending mail, appearing at petitioner's workplace, contacting petitioner by telephone, etc.);

6. Interfering with efforts to remove the aggrieved parties' child(ren) or personal property from the premises;

7. Threatening to kill or physically injure petitioner or petitioner's child(ren);

8. Interfering with petitioner at his or her place of employment or education or engaging in conduct that impairs petitioner's employment or educational relationship or environment;

9. Having access to information in records concerning a minor child of petitioner and respondent that will reveal petitioner's address, telephone number, or employment address or that will reveal the child's address or telephone number;

10. Purchasing or possessing a firearm;

11. Engaging in other behavior - as ordered by the court

While a petitioner can represent herself or himself, it would be best to seek legal counsel to assist in efforts to obtain a Personal Protection Order, since courtroom testimony usually includes direct and cross-examination of witnesses, which is best conducted by a trial attorney.

DOMESTIC VIOLENCE COUNSELING

Michigan has many domestic violence counseling agencies, which provide therapy, advocacy, help with court hearings, and emergency shelter for victims and their families. Many have 24-hour hotlines to handle crisis calls. Call the National Hotline at 1-800-799-7233 for the agency in your area. If you are abused in violation of an injunction, the assailant may be immediately arrested and brought before the judge. The judge can then impose criminal penalties such as fines, jail, or both. In my appendix see a list of shelters and agencies available, state-wide, to assist victims of domestic violence, and their children.

The court system cannot always respond quickly enough to help a family or victim stop the cycle of domestic violence.

Even with the aid of the courts, many victims and families need ongoing counseling to stop the violence.

CHILD SEXUAL ABUSE

Allegations of child sexual abuse are often made by one divorcing or divorced spouse against the other. In many cases, allegations raise justifiable concerns about a parent's behavior toward the child. However, allegations are often made without any real reason to believe they are true. False allegations of child sexual abuse are extremely damaging to the accused parent and the child. The Child Protective Services division of the Michigan Department of Human Services (formerly known as the Family Independence Agency) is equipped to investigate allegations and notify police agencies.

If you legitimately suspect that your spouse or former spouse has physically or sexually abused your child, notify Child Protective Services immediately. Also notify your attorney when you make any report to Child Protective Services. The Friend of the Court is not equipped to conduct child abuse investigations.

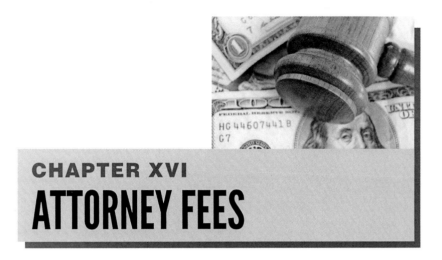

CHAPTER XVI
ATTORNEY FEES

Attorney fees must be set within the limits of the Michigan Rules of Professional Conduct (MRPC). However, the MRPC do not set actual fee levels. These are between the lawyer and the client. Both the client and the family law attorney should have a full understanding of the fee or hourly rate to be charged *before* any work is done. I charge an engagement fee based on the minimum number of hours I will have to set aside to properly represent a client in his or her particular case. When I agree to take one client's case, due to time commitments I may have to decline taking another client's case. Most lawyers will also charge a retainer fee at the beginning of the case. These engagement/retainer agreements (for court costs and attorney fees) typically range from a minimum of fifteen hundred ($1,500) to thousands of dollars, depending on the experience and reputation of the attorney **and** the anticipated complexity of the case.

In my first meeting with the client, I typically discuss the amount of the engagement fee and retainer necessary in the case, and the likely fees that may be charged. The upfront fees requested are based on an analysis of the client's facts and the unique legal issues involved in his/her case, together with the client's goals. The difficulty of obtaining the client's goals more often than not dictates the amount of the engagement fee and/or retainer requested. Both the engagement fee and the retainer fee are applied toward the client's final bill.

Should a client decide to retain my services, a written agreement will be signed by both of us, detailing our full agreement so that each of us is aware of our individual rights and responsibilities. A copy of the agreement will be given to the client, and one will be kept in the client's file in my office. Most family law attorneys utilize a written fee agreement to spell out how charges are incurred.

My attorney fees are based on a number of factors, which include:

a)   the amount and nature of the services rendered;

b)   the time, labor, and difficulty involved;

c)   the character and importance of the litigation;

d)   the number of assets and value of the marital estate affected;

e) the requisite professional skill and expertise exercised by my staff;

f) the novelty and difficulty of the legal questions involved;

g) the specific goals of the client; and

h) the results obtained.

In addition to attorney fees, there may be other charges associated with a divorce. The client is also responsible for payment of expenses such as court costs, filing fees, service of process, appraisals, expert witness fees, etc.

One spouse may be ordered to contribute to the attorney fees of the other spouse. In order to receive attorney fees from your spouse, the court must be convinced that you are unable to pay the fees yourself and that your spouse is financially able to contribute to paying for your legal fees and litigation costs.

CHAPTER XVII

RELATED ISSUES – ANNULMENT/SEPARATE MAINTENANCE

ANNULMENT

I am often asked, when there has been a marriage of short duration, whether the marriage can be annulled. There are specific advantages for annulment, mostly emotional since the party can maintain that he/she was never married, rather than divorced. Also, there may be a religious reason for seeking an annulment versus divorce.

A marriage can be annulled if it is void *ab initio,* meaning that the marriage is deemed to have never taken place at all due to the occurrence of several grounds for an annulment.

GROUNDS FOR ANNULMENT INCLUDE:

1) If one of the parties to the marriage has a prior spouse who is still living and is not divorced. This is known as bigamy.

2) Marriages between two parties related within certain degrees of consanguinity or affinity are prohibited.

3) Mental incompetence. A marriage contract, like other contracts, must be based on two individuals knowingly having the ability to enter the contract. If either is deemed to have been mentally incompetent when the marriage occurred, then the marriage can be annulled.

4) Underage marriages. Persons must be at least 18 years of age in order to enter into a marriage. If a person is over 16, but under 18, he/she may marry with the written consent of one of his or her parents having legal custody, or a legal guardian. A person under the age of 16 is incapable of marrying.

5) When a marriage occurs under duress. Again, marriage is a civil contract and if one person forces another person to marry, the lack of consent is a basis for granting an annulment.

6) In addition to duress, fraud also may be a basis for an annulment if one party fraudulently represented himself regarding an important consideration whether to marry. For example, when someone says, "I want to have children," then, after marriage, states, "I really do not want to have children."

7) A sexually transmitted disease. A person who marries when he or she has a communicable disease is incapable of contracting marriage and can actually be prosecuted criminally for the same.

8) Sterility or impotency. A marriage in which one of the parties has concealed the fact that he or she has a physical incapacity to have children continues to be valid unless the wronged party seeks a judicial decree to annul it.

9) A marriage that has not been solemnized can be set aside—when parties claim to marry as a folly or a joke, especially when under the influence of alcohol; such marriage can be set aside (assuming there has been no conjugal relations based on such a marriage).

SEPARATE MAINTENANCE

Another option for people seeking divorce is obtaining a decree of separate maintenance. An action for separate maintenance is filed in the same manner and based on the same statutory grounds as a divorce. If both parties agree, such a complaint for separate maintenance can be filed and a judgment entered when one or both of the parties is not ready to dissolve the marriage, but wants the security of having their assets divided, dealing with custody and support issues, but holding off on terminating the marriage. This option also is used by some practitioners to attempt to continue employee health care benefits for the spouses, since no divorce has occurred.

The attempt to preserve health care benefits may not work, as the health care coverage is a contract between the employer and the employee. Most health plans and retirement plans include separate maintenance as a "qualifying event" that triggers termination of benefits. Accordingly, counsel should check with each individual health plan to determine if a separate maintenance judgment is a triggering event. In such an instance, entry of a separate maintenance judgment will trigger the qualifying event and health care benefits will terminate for the non-employee spouse just as they would in the event of a divorce.

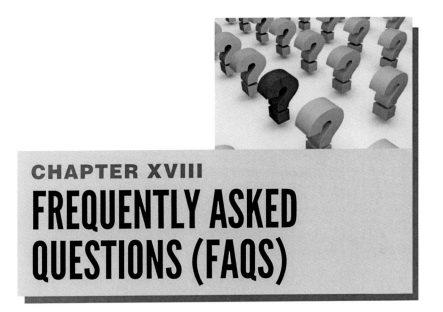

CHAPTER XVIII
FREQUENTLY ASKED QUESTIONS (FAQS)

FAQS

1. CAN I STOP MY SPOUSE FROM DIVORCING ME?

<u>**Answer:**</u> Yes and no. You can ask your spouse to stop the proceeding and offer to engage in counseling, but if the other spouse does not agree, then you can't stop him or her. Ultimately, a spouse can always obtain a divorce if that's what he or she wants to do.

2. HOW DO I PROTECT MYSELF FINANCIALLY IF I AM GOING THROUGH A DIVORCE?

Answer: Some proactive steps that you can take are:

i. Check with all stock brokerage and financial institutions where you have accounts to see if there have been any withdrawals. Ask if you can put a hold on the assets and not allow early withdrawals without your knowledge and consent;

ii. Obtain your credit report to see if there are any debts on the report that you are not aware of being incurred. Your spouse may have obtained a new credit card by forging your signature;

iii. Write down all the ways that your spouse might adversely affect your financial health to ensure that you are taking all the proactive steps you can take to make sure that this won't happen to you; and

iv. If you are very concerned, ask an attorney to file for divorce and request that the court order that no asserts owned by either you or your spouse can be sold, mortgaged, or transferred without your consent or without an order signed by the court.

3. WHAT ARE THE GROUNDS FOR A DIVORCE?

Answer: In Michigan, the sole ground for divorce is that the court must find that there has been a breakdown of the marriage relationship to the extent that the objects of matrimony have been destroyed and there remains no reasonable likelihood that the marriage can be preserved. Previously, there had to be fault found by one party, such as adultery or physical or mental abuse. Once Michigan adopted the no-fault language of our current statute, fault is no longer required as a basis for obtaining a divorce in Michigan.

While specific allegations of fault need not be set forth in the complaint for divorce, fault of one party may still be important in determining whether alimony should be awarded and whether property distribution should deviate from a typical 50/50 property split. For example, a divorce caused by the fault of one spouse may result in something other than a 50/50 property split—55/45 or 60/40. Fault may also be relevant in a child custody dispute, especially if the children have been directly affected by witnessing the inappropriate behavior or actions of the at-fault spouse. Allegations of fault, such as adultery or domestic violence, are often set forth in specific pleadings regarding alimony or custody of the parties' minor children.

4. IS THERE A TRIAL IN EVERY DIVORCE CASE?

Answer: No. In most divorce cases, there is not a trial. And in divorce cases, if a trial does take place, it is typically before a family law judge. Rarely, a tort may be alleged, and a jury trial may be sought on the issue of damages.

5. HOW MUCH WILL MY DIVORCE CASE COST IN TERMS OF ATTORNEY FEES AND EXPENSES?

Answer: There is no way to accurately project the cost of a divorce case, since the ultimate expense of obtaining a divorce will depend on many different factors. Some of those factors include the complexity of the property settlement, whether experts have to be hired, and whether appraisals have to be obtained.

Additionally, the biggest cost factor in any litigation is generated by whether the parties are able to amicably agree on issues that need to be resolved. Is there going to be a child custody dispute? Are the parties going to agree that spousal support should be paid? Is there an agreement on how to divide deferred compensation monies or a pension? Who will pay for the cost to prepare the QDRO or EDRO? Who is going to be awarded the marital home? How is credit card debt going to be split and/or who is going to pay for such debt?

If each of these issues is not able to be resolved without consternation, then the cost of the divorce will go up. I typically advise clients that the attitude of their spouse and the attitude of their spouse's attorney will determine how expensive their divorce will be. Additionally, the more experienced the divorce lawyer on the other side, the better chance that your case will be <u>less</u> expensive. Often, lawyers who do not regularly practice in the family law area drive the cost of a divorce case up, rather than down.

6. WHAT ARE THE ISSUES TYPICALLY INVOLVED IN A DIVORCE?

Answer: The issues in every divorce usually deal with property settlement and, potentially, child related issues. If there are no minor children involved, then the case is much less complicated. But even in a case without minor children, if the financial entanglements of the parties are significant, especially when there is a family-owned business involved, there still may be a multitude of issues to "equitably" divide the assets acquired and the debts incurred during the marriage.

7. I HAVE HEARD OF A LEGAL SEPARATION. WHAT IS IT?

Answer: Although a "legal separation" is not specifically authorized by any Michigan statute, the court is empowered to issue a judgment of separate maintenance. This is typically thought of as a legal separation. An action for a separate maintenance is filed in the same manner and based on the same grounds as a divorce action.

In a legal separation, property is divided and spousal support may be awarded. When the matter is concluded, however, a judgment of separate maintenance will be entered, but the parties will technically remain married. People may request a decree of separate maintenance, rather than a judgment of divorce, because they have a religious objection to a divorce, or they may want to elect to attempt to continue health coverage to a spouse who may be in need of the same. When health insurance coverage is the issue, parties need to check with the employer's health care insurance company to make sure that the company's policy allows for coverage to continue in such a situation (many insurance companies do not allow coverage to continue).

8. I HAVE HEARD THAT THERE ARE TWO TYPES OF CHILD CUSTODY. WHAT DOES THAT MEAN?

Answer: Yes, there are two types of child custody. One is known as "legal custody" and that is having the right to have input on the important decisions that affect the parties' minor children. Such important discussions include whether the minor children can have an elective medical procedure, what church or school they will attend, what extra-curricular activities the child can participate in, and whether they can marry at age 16. Legal custody may either be joint or sole to one party.

The other type of custody is "physical custody." Again, such custody describes who is the primary custodial parent.

Custody may either be primarily with the mother, the father, a third party, or joint with both parents or with one parent and a third party. Even though the parties may share physical custody, that does not necessarily mean that the children spend exactly the same amount of time with each parent. For example, with joint physical custody, one parent might have the children ten out of every 14 nights and the custody relationship might still be described by the parties as joint physical custody. Some parents can also agree to include grandparents or some other third party into the custody arrangement or into a parenting time agreement.

9. HOW IS PARENTING TIME DIFFERENT FROM CUSTODY?

Answer: Parenting time spells out when the children will be with each parent. Typically, parenting time is geared around where the children spend overnights with one parent versus the other parent. However, parenting time can also include where the children will be after school and during specific time periods on weekends. Parenting time agreements could say, for instance, that the children will go to their mother's or father's house after school between 3:00 and 4:00 pm and remain there until 7:00 pm each night when they are picked up by their mother or father. Parenting times are typically spelled out in the parties' judgment of divorce, and may also include provisions to make such parenting time flexible. During the school year, most parenting time schedules revolve around a 14-day schedule. In unique cases, third parties, including grandparents, can also be provided with parenting time.

10. DOES ALIMONY STILL EXIST IN MICHIGAN?

Answer: Yes. Alimony refers to support paid by a former spouse to the other. The purpose of alimony is to help one spouse meet his or her financial needs after divorce, because he or she is unable to fully provide for his or her own support. In Michigan, there are 14 factors that the court considers when deciding whether to award alimony or spousal support. At the top of the list is the need of the party requesting the alimony and the financial ability of the other spouse to pay alimony. Is one spouse earning substantially more than the other spouse so that he or she can afford to pay spousal support? The length of the marriage is the other most important factor. The longer the marriage, the more likely the court will order spousal support. The age of the parties is also a very important factor. The health of the parties can be a very important factor if one party is physically unable to work. The older a party is who is requesting support, the more likely the court will aid that party to at least reach retirement age. But there are many other factors that the court takes into consideration, and an experienced family law attorney needs to carefully evaluate all factors when analyzing a case for alimony.

11. HOW MUCH CHILD SUPPORT WILL I HAVE TO PAY OR CAN I EXPECT TO RECEIVE IN MY DIVORCE?

Answer: This is a complicated question that requires a careful analysis. In Michigan, we have adopted a child support formula to establish what amount of child support will normally be ordered in a case. The formula takes into consideration the income of each spouse and the number of overnights that the children will be spending with one spouse versus the other. Deviations from the formula can occur if equity and good conscience call for the same, such as when the parties have agreed to a disproportionate property settlement, e.g. when the marital home has been given by one spouse to the other in exchange for reducing the child support obligation. Again, careful analysis needs to be made by an experienced family law attorney to determine what amount of child support is likely to be ordered, and if there exist reasons to deviate from the amount recommended by the state's formula.

12. ARE PRE-NUPTIAL (POST-NUPTIAL) AGREEMENTS HONORED IN MICHIGAN?

Answer: Currently, Michigan recognizes pre-nuptial (also known as ante-nuptial) and likely post-nuptial agreements, as binding in the event that the parties end up in divorce. That being said, however, such agreements need to be carefully drawn and should only be entered into with the advice of legal counsel. Although it is not specifically required, it is better to have both parties represented by independent legal counsel. As in the case of divorce, one lawyer cannot ethically represent both the bride and the groom in regard to advising the parties on the ramifications of such an agreement.

Currently, a Michigan Court of Appeals decision (Wright v. Wright) held that Michigan does not permit post-nuptial agreements. This author is confident, however, that such a blanket statement is not actually the state of the law in Michigan. The judge who authored Wright v. Wright has stated at more than one family law seminar that if given the opportunity to do so, he would re-examine the holding; he believes that the law would be more to the effect that post-nuptial agreements, like pre-nuptial agreements, will be carefully looked at to ensure that both parties negotiated such an agreement with their eyes open, were not pressured into signing such an agreement, and—like any enforceable contract—that there was sufficient consideration given to both parties at the time of entering into such an agreement.

Pre-nuptial agreements need to contain specific provisions for both parties that effectively define each party's rights in the event of a divorce or the death of a party during marriage. They should also describe which assets are to be marital assets and which assets are not to be deemed marital assets in the event of a divorce. Assets and debts have to be listed and fully disclosed to both parties. In order to enter into a prenuptial agreement, parties should contact legal counsel well in advance of the anticipated marriage to allow for careful consideration of all of the issues involved. If a prenuptial or post-nuptial agreement is found to be valid, then such an agreement will control the division of marital assets at the time of divorce.

CHAPTER XIX
EPILOGUE

This book was prepared to provide you with a better understanding of the divorce process in Michigan. In compiling this book, I drew much of my information from court rules, Michigan statutes, Michigan family law journals and publications, court decisions, and years of experience in dealing with parents and children going through times of crisis. Many of the suggestions contained herein have come from other family law practitioners and although no attribution is given, I thank those individuals for their suggestions and request their indulgence in my utilization of such suggestions. I have attempted to highlight the areas of greatest concern for most Michigan residents with the understanding that a greater explanation and elaboration of the process during a meeting with any client will be given to that client based on the unique facts of such client's marriage.

Divorce is an increasingly complex process—legally, financially, and emotionally. Although it is possible to pursue a divorce on your own without an attorney, if a party does so, he/she runs the risk of losing important rights in all but the simplest of cases.

In order to provide clients with the best representation available, it is important that the client communicate to his/her attorney all of the information that relates to his or her divorce. Any fact that a party fails to discuss with his/her attorney could seriously undermine his/her case.

If, after reading this book, you have additional questions or concerns, you are encouraged to contact my office to schedule an appointment for a consultation with me or a member of my staff. You can certainly also contact any experienced family law attorney in your local area and request an initial consultation with him or her, to have your additional questions addressed.

When clients contact my office staff requesting a consultation, a one-half hour initial consultation is scheduled for them at a nominal charge. At this meeting, I typically meet with the potential new client and offer advice regarding the unique facts about his or her situation that cannot be addressed in a book of this general nature.

As an experienced family law attorney, if I have a consultation with you, I will endeavor to be a good listener to your special and unique problems and do everything in my power to help you keep your separation process as amicable as possible. I will also keep in mind the financial costs to you and your spouse and the emotional aspects of your case. My aim is to keep the divorce process as plain and simple as possible—but to make sure your rights and the best interests of your minor children are paramount.

If your spouse is treating you and your children fairly, with dignity, and respecting your rights, then he or she will also be respected by me as your attorney. If, on the other hand, your spouse is abusing you, is attempting to bully you, is being dishonest with you, or is trying to hide assets from you then, if I represent you, your spouse may not like me, as I will not allow you or your children to be treated in such a manner.

That being said, I always start out the divorce process, especially where minor children are involved, with the belief that when you and your spouse married, you once loved each other, and that the woman continues to be the children's mother and that the man continues to be their father. In such regard, unless the other spouse engages in behavior harmful to my client or my client's minor children, my approach when representing my client is always to be respectful of my client's spouse, even though at least one of the parties has chosen to divorce.

ABOUT THE AUTHOR

Mr. Barberi has practiced law in the Central Michigan area for over thirty years. For twelve years, Mr. Barberi served as Prosecuting Attorney for Isabella County. Mr. Barberi is a graduate of Central Michigan University and a cum laude graduate of the Detroit College of Law, which is now Michigan State University College of Law. Mr. Barberi ranked 5th in his graduating class of 241 students.

Mr. Barberi has been recognized by his peers, having been appointed by the Michigan Supreme Court to serve on a committee revising Michigan's Court Rules. While serving as Prosecuting Attorney for Isabella County, he was elected by his fellow prosecutors to serve as their president of the Prosecuting Attorneys Association of Michigan (PAAM). Mr. Barberi is also past president of the Isabella County Bar Association. Readers of Central Michigan University's (*CM*

Life) newspaper, and the Mt. Pleasant morning newspaper, *The Morning Sun*, have voted Mr. Barberi as the #1 attorney in the Central Michigan area for twelve years in a row (2000-2012).

For over twenty years, Mr. Barberi has been a member of the Michigan Family Law Section of the Michigan State Bar and has been a regular attendee of numerous Family Law and Matrimonial Law seminars and workshops. Mr. Barberi has also been a presenter at trial technique seminars for the Michigan Association for Justice (MAJ) and Prosecuting Attorneys Association of Michigan (PAAM).

Mr. Barberi is well known as a successful trial lawyer in the Central Michigan area. Mr. Barberi has tried over 300 jury trials and only lost three. Mr. Barberi is known for his expertise in the area of child custody proceedings and grandparent (grandchild) rights.

Mr. Barberi and his capable staff of paralegals and associate attorneys employ a team approach, assigning two attorneys (one of whom is Mr. Barberi) and at least one paralegal to every family law case. This approach allows Mr. Barberi to handle a number of contested divorce cases at the same time, while making sure that each client receives the individual attention that his or her case requires. Mr. Barberi is well known for his passion in divorce and custody cases and for taking every case personally.

IMPORTANT DISCLAIMER

THE DIVORCE BOOK:

What Every Married MICHIGAN Man or Woman Needs to Know

This is an informational consumer guide intended to assist the public. It is not legal advice. It is written as general information and is not a substitute for informed professional legal, psychiatric, psychological, tax, investment, accounting, counseling, or other professional advice. Laws change, court decisions interpreting and changing case precedent occur weekly; all of these changes can cause advice to change as well, even advice based on the same facts.

Some observant readers may come across a fact or two that might appear to be in error. They may consider writing me to point out such observations. In our world, my advice is we should all try to save trees (paper). There are mistakes in this book, as with most books. No matter how hard one tries to avoid mistakes—mistakes will always occur. My hope is that such unintended error will be insignificant in nature, and that those observant readers finding error will be both understanding and forgiving.

Accordingly, comments and opinions set forth in this book should neither be relied on as legal advice, nor professional advice of any other kind. Reading this book does not create an attorney/client relationship between the author and the reader. In order to receive proper legal advice or professional advice of any kind, an individual needs to discuss his or her unique facts with a professional who, at that time, will then be in a position to give the client or patient, his or her best professional advice.

PLEASE REFER A FRIEND TO GET OUR FREE NEWSLETTERS

If you are reading this book, you might also be getting our newsletter. (If not, call us and we'll sign you up.) Now, you can get this newsletter for all of your friends. In our newsletter you can read interesting stories about the law and other news items that we believe you will find very useful.

There is no need to destroy this book. Just photocopy this form, fill it out and mail or fax it to us. Fax to (989) 772-6444 or mail to Joseph T. Barberi, P.C., 2305 Hawthorn Drive, Ste C, Mt. Pleasant, MI 48858. Or send us a list of names and we'll send them the newsletter, along with a note telling them that you've helped make it available to them. Don't worry, we don't spam! If they don't want to get it, there is always a toll-free number to use to get off the free subscription list.

☐ **PLEASE START MY SUBSCRIPTION TO YOUR FREE LEGAL NEWSLETTER**

Name: _____

Address: _____

City: _____ State: ___ Zip: _____

Email address: _____

IF YOU WOULD LIKE ANOTHER COPY OF THIS BOOK

If others want a free copy of this book, or you want an additional copy to give to a friend, simply fill out the form below and mail it to us, and we will send you or them a free copy to whatever address you give us.

If confidentiality is an issue, you can pick up a copy at our law office at Joseph T. Barberi, P.C., 2305 Hawthorn Drive, Ste C, Mt. Pleasant, MI 48858, or order an e-version from us. Copies can also be ordered at Amazon.com, but there is a $16.95 sales price!

SEND ME A FREE COPY OF MR. BARBERI'S BOOK, "THE DIVORCE BOOK: WHAT EVERY MICHIGAN MARRIED MAN OR WOMAN NEEDS TO KNOW"

Name: _____

Address: _____

City: _____ State: _____ Zip: _____

Email address: _____